ZEN AND THE
ART OF
KNITTING

Exploring the Links Between Knitting,
Spirituality, and Creativity

Bernadette Murphy

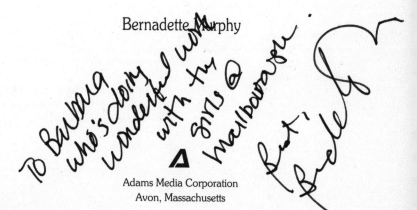

Adams Media Corporation
Avon, Massachusetts

Published by
Adams Media Corporation
57 Littlefield Street, Avon, MA 02322 U.S.A.
www.adamsmedia.com

ISBN: 1-58062-654-8

Printed in Canada.

J I H G F E D C B A

Library of Congress Cataloging-in-Publication-Data
Murphy, Bernadette.
Zen and the art of knitting : exploring the links between knitting,
spirituality, and creativity / by Bernadette Murphy.
p.   cm.
ISBN 1-58062-654-8
1. Knitting. 2. Spiritual life--Zen Buddhism. I. Title.
TT820 .M87 2002
746.43'2--dc21
2002008608

This publication is designed to provide accurate and authoritative information with
regard to the subject matter covered. It is sold with the understanding that the publisher
is not engaged in rendering legal, accounting, or other professional advice. If legal
advice or other expert assistance is required, the services of a competent professional
person should be sought.

—From a *Declaration of Principles* jointly adopted
by a Committee of the American Bar Association
and a Committee of Publishers and Associations

Illustrations by Eric Andrews.

This book is available at quantity discounts for bulk purchases.
For information, call 1-800-872-5627.

Table of Contents

Acknowledgments v
Introduction vii

chapter one   Knitting Myself Back Together 1
chapter two   Feeding the Soul   19
chapter three   Resting the Mind 35
chapter four   Ripening the Intellect   59
chapter five   Contented Soul 85
chapter six   Creative Spirit 111
chapter seven   Wise Heart   139
chapter eight   Warming the Body 159
chapter nine   Grateful Nature 167
chapter ten   Of a Piece 189

How to Get Started 197
Basic Get-Going Pattern 205
Index 209

For my mother,
in whose womb my being was knit.

Acknowledgments

I'd like to thank all the knitters who shared their stories with me and all the friends of friends who said, "I know a knitter you should talk to." Without their generous sharing and openness, this book would not be possible.

A legion of non-knitters helped me as well: Bonnie Nadell believed in this project when it was little more than an idea and provided the encouragement to see it through. My editor, Kate Epstein, saved me from myself a number of times; responsibility for any errors in the final book, though, belongs squarely with me. The intrepid ladies of my Tao group—Kate, Cathy, Michelle, and Tracy—bucked me up every Tuesday night throughout the writing process, and my brother Brendan created the illustrations for each chapter when he'd much rather have been working on his own art; to them I owe a deep debt of gratitude. I am especially indebted to the members of my writing circle, particularly Marjorie Gellhorn Sa'adah, Tara Ison, Michelle Huneven, Kitty Nard, and David L. Ulin: you are my heroes.

To my family—John, Jarrod, Neil, and Hope Fasching—who, by nature of their relationship with me, are stuck putting up with the vicissitudes of this writer's life: I'd be lost without you.

Introduction

Knitting a sweater is a tremendous act of faith. One undertakes an ancient practice that requires hundreds of thousands of hand-wrought stitches and hours upon hours of concentration to translate and follow pattern instructions that seem written in an archaic language, or to create something completely new. Throughout, it's a tentative process. At any point, a firm tug on an unsecured piece of yarn could unravel the entire work. Because knitting uses no knots, every stitch is little more than a twisted and twined bit of yarn, each section a group of simple but tenuous webs. When the work is finished, though, those webs coalesce into a garment rugged enough to withstand a lifetime of wear.

It is in this tension—between the rigid and the provisional—that knitting best reflects the complexities of human life. As a metaphor for understanding the web of unity connecting all life, and as a practice that puts one in touch with the simultaneous fragility and strength of life, knitting is both expansive and fertile.

Knitting is a process craft. Anyone who sets out to knit with the sole objective of wearing the finished work will soon be disappointed. If the finished piece were the sole aim, one would purchase a mass-produced garment at a local mall for a fraction of the cost and time required to make a sweater. The true joy comes from discovering the individual beauty of each segment, the feeling of accomplishment when completing a particularly difficult section, and the sense of challenge that lurks as you plan the next project. In other words, knitting is like life. We have to enjoy the journey if we expect the destination to mean much.

Best of all, knitting is slow. So slow that we see the beauty inherent in every tiny act that makes up a sweater. So slow that we know the project's not going to get finished today—it may not get finished for many months or longer—and thus, we make our peace with the unresolved nature of life. We slow down as we knit. Our breathing and heart rate drop and knitters who've been at it a while experience a trancelike state that provides the same benefits as other forms of meditation.

Unlike other forms of meditation, though, when all is said and done, knitting produces a beautiful, handcrafted, wearable work of art. Each garment reflects its unique moment in time and is as singular in its construction as the person who knit it—an image of its creator's spirit.

When I set out to write this book, the process was not unlike that of knitting a sweater. First, I gathered the wool I'd need. Using the Internet, telephone, and in-person meetings, I interviewed scores of knitters from around the nation about their experiences. Though knitting has provided me with great insights into life, spirituality, creativity, and art, I've only experienced a handful of the many ways knitting can enhance a life. Thus, I relied on the stories of these wonderful, generous knitters to fill in the gaps where my experience was lacking. The stories people told and wrote were enlightening, thoughtful, funny, open-hearted, and always rich in intelligence and texture.

There are as many reasons why people knit as there are types of stitches and sweater designs. Some like the connection knitting gives them to their grandmothers, aunts, mothers, and other loved ones. Many cite health benefits and relaxation as the primary reason. Others knit for fun and the sheer love of working with fibers and colors. Some recognize the spiritual and meditative qualities of their handwork while others see the craft as only a hobby. Many knit to find a sense of their own uniqueness in their often busy lives, to be reminded that they, too, are creative beings.

Most of the knitters I interviewed were women, though I did speak to some men. Why knitting predominately attracts women, I'm not sure; certainly our culture seems more open to women who knit than men. I hope we'll see this change in coming years as the benefits of knitting gain recognition. For now, the scope of women who knit is astounding. I spoke with some of the most nonstereotypical knitters imaginable: highly educated women who are also doctors, psychologists, attorneys, and business owners; women who hold high-profile positions in the corporate world; knitters who are also professional artists—painters, sculptors, musicians, actors, and writers—as well as the types of knitters that most frequently come to mind: mothers, grandmothers, teachers, people interested in traditional handwork and who might be considered "crafty." Every person brought unique insight and perspective to the discussion at hand, demonstrating again and again the elastic singularity of human experience.

Once I'd gathered my material, the book's narrative grew sweaterlike: I cast on for the body with my own experience, then wove together the personal stories and reflections of those I'd interviewed. I used other knitters' expertise in the same way I might refer to a pattern book or a sweater I'd seen—to copy the decreases, say, or to be inspired by the texture, or to discover a new way of mixing colors—in order to custom-craft this narrative.

My objective was to give a broader picture of what it means to knit than what our culture commonly accepts today and to expose the creative and spiritual benefits of knitting that are not commonly known, to explore the more metaphysical and esoteric elements of this craft.

I remember seeing a television commercial that highlighted all the couch-potato kind of activities your life might be reduced to unless you consume orange juice and "get a life." The ad featured a grandmother in a rocking chair, knitting. This, to illustrate all the presumably boring activities that will be yours if you live an orange-juice-free life. From my personal experience and the fascinating stories I heard in interviews, I can tell you that such a limited view of knitters does not hold true. Yes, there

are grandmother knitters in rocking chairs—thank God for them
and the generosity with which they've passed on their craft
knowledge—but there are many more, as varied as the population of this country.

I live in Los Angeles, where knitting is the current rage
among hipsters, where edgy twentysomethings line up at fancy
knitwear design boutiques to take lessons. Yet I also encountered knitters who are radically conservative—politically, reli-
giously, and aesthetically—including one woman who refused
to be interviewed because the word "Zen" in the book's title
was antithetical to her conservative Christian philosophy. There
are feminist knitters, agnostic knitters, Jewish knitters, Buddhist
knitters; I interviewed a Pagan knitter and one who is a Wiccan
practitioner. I spoke with knitters who are recovering addicts
and alcoholics as well as knitting nuns and priests. Women told
me stories of knitting to ease heartbreak, knitting as a tool for
battling anxiety, knitting to cope with serious illness, and knitting to access higher consciousness. There were also the more
predictable yet equally valid reasons to knit: preparing for a
baby's birth; showing the special people in one's life how much
they are valued; and passing time in doctors' offices and during
kids' music lessons.

As the narrative of this book took shape, I felt the same joy
and wonder I feel when I can see how a sweater's going to look.
I've used the richest colors I could find, the organic wool of
human experience, and plied that wool with the patience necessary to recognize the small blessings that knitting provides. While
writing each section, I've tried to stay open to jabs of inspiration,

just as I'd do in knitting each piece of a sweater, praying throughout for goodness and blessings on those who receive the work of my hands. Whether you are a lifelong avid knitter or just curious about this ancient craft, I hope this narrative will enrich your life and give you a deeper sense of the sacredness inherent in knitting, as well as in all aspects of daily life.

chapter one

Knitting Myself Back Together

Simple Knit Stitch

Making a stitch is the basic action of knitting. The knitter accomplishes this using two needles. The work begins with loops formed on the left-hand needle. As the knitter makes each stitch, he tightens the loop at the stitch's base, making a provisional knot. In the process of making a stitch, the knitter moves the original loop from the left-hand needle to the right-hand needle, one stitch at a time. When all the stitches have been moved from the left needle to the right, the knitter switches hands and begins the process again. Each time this is accomplished, a row has been completed.

Unraveling

It was in Ireland during a wet November, a time when dampness seemed to camp out in my bones, that I learned to knit. It
was a place where warmth didn't offer itself freely. In that climate, a hand-knit woolen sweater became, for me, a celebrated
gift, a symbol of warmth, a garment that bucked me up and
reminded me of the tenacity of life.

I'd arrived in my ethnic homeland, a college student on
leave from school, away from my friends and immediate family;
I was alone in the world for the first time. As a twenty-one-year-
old Southern California native, I'd never spent a non-summer
season anywhere but sunlit Los Angeles and was unprepared
for the cold weather. I'd never owned rain boots, a pair of mittens, or even a muffler; I'd never seen sleet or snow falling. I
packed for my four-month sojourn on the Emerald Isle thinking
the mercury couldn't possibly drop much lower than the arctic
65 degrees of an L.A. winter.

I was wrong.

Life had delivered some blows in the preceding year. My
first boyfriend, a man with whom I'd idly discussed marriage
and viewed in that hazy, maybe-someday-in-the-future, happily-
ever-after light, had died of a drug overdose. His body had
been found, dumped in an ambulance parking lot; he was
twenty-three years old.

On the Christmas Day following his death, my mother died
of lung cancer. The blood and life force seeped out of her pores
as she moved the oxygen mask aside to plead for another

cigarette. Muzak Christmas carols played overhead. My mother had suffered from mental illness and had been absent from much of my childhood, living either in mental institutions or hidden away in the depths of her suffering. In the wake of her death, my memories of her were colored by the manic-depressive episodes and her desire to stop living. "Only the good die young," she used to tell me, only half in jest. I wanted to miss her and to feel sad that she was gone. Often, I did not. Like the Ireland I went to visit without a warm coat, I didn't know how to outfit myself for these losses.

My solution? Run away to a new land where everything would be a welcome diversion from the abiding sense of loss, a way of focusing on a new geography, a new people, a new life. The prospect of a fresh set of faces, different roads to navigate from the wrong side of the street, challenges that were unfamiliar to rouse me from the starkly ironic sunshine of California, seemed wholly worthwhile.

In going to Ireland, I was actually running right into the heart of my loss, though I didn't know it yet. Both my parents had emigrated from Dublin a quarter of a century earlier; my entire extended family lived there. In rediscovering my cousins and uncles and aunts—the very soil of my parents— how could I have thought that I'd escape the loss of my mother?

I went to stay with my aunt Peggy, my mother's oldest sister, in her small semidetached home in Churchtown, a suburb on the south side of Dublin, with enough American Express Traveler's Checks composed of saved cocktail-waitressing tips to live comfortably for a few months. I arrived with no intention of learning to knit, no intentions whatsoever except to forget as much as possible. But then, life has a strange way of giving us, if not exactly what we think we want, then what we most genuinely need.

Prior to the trip, I had been majoring in dance at college. The physicality of dance was something magical that I desperately needed: the way the discipline of the body lends itself to a parallel discipline of the mind. The activity rooted me so completely in my physical being that I was blissfully unable to focus on anything outside of the moment. It's hard to be distraught when you keep your body working and working and working. On some level, I think I confused physical exhaustion with serenity. But no matter. Dance kept me active, held the unpleasant thoughts at bay, and I'd enjoyed performing, the previous years in California, with a regional repertory dance company.

When the newness of Ireland wore off and I found myself alone with an elderly aunt and little in the way of distraction, resuming dance classes seemed logical. I started taking the bus into downtown Dublin two nights a week with my bag of leotards and tights slung over my shoulder. Soon, I was asked to join "Loose Connections," a dance company that performed at local pubs and publicity events.

We rehearsed in the second-story studio space of the dance school. The dampness of the climate mixed with the heat of our sweating bodies served to fog up not only the windows looking down on the fashionable shoppers on Grafton Street but even the mirrors themselves, making it impossible to follow dance moves in the reflected surface. I was mesmerized by our ability to choreograph and train when we could scarcely see what we were doing.

I had no trouble fitting in with the rest of the dance company since my entire gene pool was pretty much the same as theirs. I'd already experienced the shocked reactions of my cousin's friends upon hearing my accent for the first time—"You're a Yank!" So I didn't speak much, which made it easier to blend in.

In late October, the dance company was scheduled to bring in a crowd at a newly opened pub in Black Rock on the outskirts of Dublin. On the ride to the pub, the other dancers figured out that I was a foreigner. Once in the dressing room, they toasted me with Malibu, a syrupy-tasting rum they envisioned as a classic West Coast drink. *"Slainté!"* They lifted the bottle in a Gaelic toast for a second round. "To California!" They poured a third.

The music came up and it was time for us to take the stage. The first number went off well—lots of shoulder shimmies, heads of hair flailing about on necks barely attached to bodies. The second number is lost to my memory, but the third one, which began with a series of arduous leaps, has engraved itself in my mind: the feel of my left foot repeatedly receiving my entire body's weight with nothing but an unforgiving brass floor to help it, the sense that my leaps might be fine but that my leg wasn't, the swirl of sweating dancer-faces and jutting limbs in the smoky room. I argued with myself that everything was as it should be, that the off-kilter sensation was just an effect of the rum.

But it was more than the rum. By the time the show was over, I couldn't walk without help. I applied ice to my swelling ankle and calf, propped on a barstool, and drank more rum, fig-uring the swelling would go down by morning.

The next day I hobbled to the bus stop, on my way to the Physiotherapy Sports Medicine Center in downtown Dublin, where I learned I had a damaged Achilles tendon and a severe case of sciatica brought on by a pinched nerve in my lower spine. I was lucky, they told me. I wouldn't need surgery. I also wouldn't walk properly for nearly two months, and I would never dance professionally again.

There's something at once terrifying and wonderful when life strips away preconceived notions of how things are sup-posed to work out. You can keep protesting—No, that isn't fair, that's not the plan!—but at a certain point, all protestation becomes mute. I was at the horrible, jarring, do-anything-to-avoid-it moment of surrender.

Looking for a Spiritual Path

Aunt Peggy was nearing seventy, a slender, frail-looking woman with crooked fingers, a pointy nose, and cat's-eye glasses that she wore with absolutely no irony, her eyes cloudy through the unwiped lenses. She favored simple plaid skirts in pastel colors with stockings and low-heeled pumps. A cardigan of spotless white draped her shoulders like an altar cloth.

Aunt Peggy attended daily mass. Similar to my parents, she was staunchly, conservatively, dyed-in-the-wool Catholic. A single mother with two grown children—the first lived next door to her, the second, the door next to that—Aunt Peggy organized rosary times for the kids in the neighborhood and personally led these sessions in her living room, which she had converted into a kind of chapel. Pictures of the Sacred Heart of Jesus and Pope John Paul II, together with a calligraphy-rendered Prayer of St. Francis and a shrine to Our Lady, were the room's central decor. The scent of blown-out candles mixed with the must of disuse and copious amounts of dusting spray. Though Aunt Peggy hadn't traveled widely, she'd made a pilgrimage to Vatican City and to Lourdes, where The Immaculate Conception visited St. Bernadette, my namesake and that of my mother. She had bottles of Lourdes water on hand at all times for medical needs—a small traveling bottle nestled in her purse—believing absolutely in the healing power of this water.

I no longer knew where I fit in this continuum of faith. I no longer knew where I fit anywhere. I'd tried for years to recapture the innocent belief of my childhood, and in Ireland, though I went to daily mass with Aunt Peggy when my leg felt up to it and occasionally participated in her rosary group, hoping that something dormant in me might reawaken, nothing much shook loose.

The spiritual path chosen by my parents and Aunt Peggy never inspired me the way I'd hoped. The grudges I held, most surrounding what I saw as a conspiracy of silence, stood in the way. Like my parents, Aunt Peggy didn't believe in discussing the disappointments of life that, like shards of glass buried under the skin, irritated and burned. In their cosmology, calamity was a path to God, something to be "offered up" in speechless obedience and used as a catalyst for yet greater spiritual development. To do what *I* wanted—pull apart the tragedies and try to make some sense of them, talk and write about them until the ache dissolved in the well of shared humanity—made me a Doubting Thomas, one with too little faith.

Likewise, I balked at the church's urging of confession as the path to inner healing because I'd watched my mother race back to the priest time and again, hoping that making a "good" confession would remove her mental affliction. I'd often wished that her worries—those weights that haunted her mind and sent her boomeranging to the confessional, those things she was unable to "offer up"—could have been discussed in the light of day, not just in that hushed-up, dark seclusion. I believed she went to her death thinking her mental illness was a sign that she hadn't been faithful enough, somehow.

Beginning

Stuck at Aunt Peggy's, I'd searched the house in vain for something interesting to read and grew bored with the American programs that filled the two television stations. Aunt Peggy, sensing the awkwardness between us, looked for some common ground.

"Let's go through the box of old family photos stored in the chapel room," she suggested, turning on the electric fireplace to warm the hallowed space, which was as cold and still as a walk-in freezer. The electric heater was meant to replicate a roaring fireplace, but with its orange coils that buzzed like a refrigerator set behind charred-looking imitation logs, it made me wonder if the person who designed it had ever seen a real fire in action. I kept my thoughts to myself because Aunt Peggy loved this little fake fire—the ease with which she could light and extinguish it, the messless quality of its buzzing heat, the way it represented a simple comfort. The heater did its job of warming the room, though, and as we dug through the cardboard box, fishing out mismatched and sequenceless photographs, we pulled our chairs a little closer to the buzzing source of warmth.

There were a handful of photos featuring my mother when she lived in Ireland, long before I was born, back when she was happy.

"Here she is, singing in the band. That's your father, there, third from the left with the trombone." Peggy held up the old black-and-white, poking at it with her twisted forefinger.

Then there were the later pictures, sent by my mother to her older sister, featuring me and my four siblings, dirty-faced kids basking in the never-ending sun of Los Angeles. My mother was in almost none of these.

"That's the blow-up swimming pool we set up every summer, and in the corner you can see the swing set. I'm pretending to be a scuba diver." I narrated the scenes, hoping she'd ask why my mother wasn't in any of the pictures.

She didn't.

Peggy and I had never talked about my mother's mental illness, and I couldn't seem to bring up the subject, though my chest burned with desire for confirmation. One of the hazards of not talking about the happenings of your life is that you start to doubt your version of events. I believed that my mother was not in any of the pictures because she was in one of the mental institutions that had inscribed my childhood or that she had run away from home once again—"I have to get away from you children!"—at the time the photo was snapped. But there was nowhere to turn for corroboration. My mother's illness, like many things, was a subject of discussion unofficially forbidden at home. I wasn't sure if that edict was enforced on this side of the icy Atlantic, but I was too afraid to test it.

We held up pictures for each other to see—black-and-whites that were glossy and crisp, color photos that had faded with age, some torn and crumpled, faces we couldn't decipher—not talking about the electroshock treatments and how my mother would forget her children for a day or two afterwards. Never mentioning the psychotropic drugs with which she'd repeatedly overdosed. It's not that Aunt Peggy had been kept in the dark about her sister's illness. Peggy knew the history as well as I, but she was able to do what I could not: offer it up.

We came across a picture of me when I was about ten. I was holding knitting needles and a big skein of acrylic red yarn.

"I didn't know you knit," Aunt Peggy said. "Did your mother teach you?"

I didn't know I knit either, though a shaky memory of learning knit and purl in Girl Scouts started to form. I thought about her question for a moment, wanting Aunt Peggy to remember nice things about her sister and wishing for a mother-daughter memory that I could hold onto.

"Yes," I lied. "She taught me and we used to sit around and knit together, though I was never very good at it."

At that, we put away the box of photos and pulled out instead a basket of knitting supplies. Aunt Peggy selected thick beige wool and fat needles for my fumbling fingers, casting on enough stitches so that I could relearn the basics without making too much of a mess. She retrieved a lilac cardigan-in-process that had been languishing.

"I started this six months ago and it's still here," she said, shaking her head. "It's time to get it done."

Learning to knit is one of the most awkward activities one will ever undertake as an adult. Like a stroke victim who has to relearn so many everyday tasks, you think all the while, "Why is this so difficult? Look at how easy it is for everyone else. Surely I should be able to do this." Every digit feels like a swollen thumb, your hands don't like feel your own—more like they've mutinied and failed to inform your brain. You're a four-year-old trying to tie impossible-to-understand shoelaces.

I remembered close to nothing about my adolescent attempts at knitting and now followed Aunt Peggy's moves, step by step by step, asking her to slow down to a snail's pace so that I could see what she was doing. The metal needles felt cold in my hands; the wool became tangled around me.

Two hours later, though, I could make a stitch by myself; the basic knit/purl concept was starting to make sense. *Insert the needle. Wind yarn around clockwise. Don't let go of needles. Pull the stitch through. Take it off the needle . . . Now the next one.*

Finally I could do a row or two without having to stop and ask Aunt Peggy for help. The needles were warm. I could see the difference between the knit side and the purl. *Insert needle. Wind yarn.* Though my attention was riveted on what I was doing and my shoulders were scrunched up in knots with the effort, I began to notice a subtle change in my aunt. *Don't let go of needles.* Her brittle awkwardness seemed to have left her, the jutting chin and pinprick eyes had relaxed into a gentle softness I'd never seen before. *Take the stitch off.* We remained ensconced in her shrine room throughout the afternoon and evening, that silly heater pumping out insignificant quantities of warmth, unable to talk in any genuine way about the person we had in common, but knitting ourselves across the chasm that divided us nonetheless. . . . *Now the next stitch.*

Two weeks later, after hours and hours of painstaking, laboriously slow stitch making—what else was I going to do?—my knitting looked atrocious.

Aunt Peggy let me know. "Couldn't you see that was a purl row? Just look at it, would you! How could you think it was meant for knit?" But as she took the snarled knitting from my hands and ripped out my work of the previous hour, she erased my mistakes and expertly replaced every stitch in just the right order so that I could start again. It was a wonderful, painful experience, to see how blunders could be redone, to learn that when I messed up, and messed up in a big way, I could go back to the place before the mistake and correct it. That's not to say that I was having fun. I wanted to scream with frustration *every* time she found my "glaring" errors (though I still couldn't see them), but for some reason, I trusted her and the process.

Eventually, Aunt Peggy deemed my stitches respectable enough to warrant a proper project. We took the bus into Dublin one day when I had to go into town for physical therapy and stopped by the knitting department of Marks & Spencer. I wanted to make a sweater for my newly widowed father, something to warm his heart after the loss he'd incurred. I walked the department, picking up skeins of wool, holding each in my hand for weight and then rubbing the favorite ones against my cheek, inhaling the sense of the sheep from which they'd come, luxuriating in the myriad textures and colors. We chose a simple pullover v-neck vest as the pattern, a pair of wooden needles, and a chunky forest green wool that had just a nice amount of itch.

"It'll knit up quickly," Aunt Peggy assured me.

What seemed quick to her was like a lifetime to me. I cast on 96 stitches, having to count and recount five times until I was sure I had the correct number. I made 3 inches of ribbing (knit one, purl one, all the way across) and then started on the body. I messed up a few times, had to rip out and replace my work, and then suddenly, I was holding something real and tangible in my hands. Not a sampler. Not a bunch of clumped-up knots or a pathetic dishcloth, but the beginning of a genuine sweater. I stuck at it, two steps forward, one step back, ripping out stitches when she found the mistake I'd made three rows earlier. As I worked on my preschooler-type project, Peggy whipped up cardigans and pullovers, beautiful

Aran designs sliding off her fingers as easily as she prayed the rosary.

The magic started when I began to shape the neck of my father's pullover. I found myself giving in to the trance, relaxing deeply though my fingers were still at work. I was no longer thinking of each stitch, but trusting my hands to know what to do. My mind drifted at first, and then thoughts of my mother bubbled up, unbidden. I wasn't afraid of them now; they surrounded me, like old friends keeping me company. I told her that I was sorry she was gone and that I hoped she was happy now. That I was sorry she hadn't had a more normal life and that I forgave her.

I knitted on and thought of my father, trying to say with each stitch I made the phrases I couldn't say aloud: that I loved him, even though we couldn't talk about much; that I wished he could see me the way that I was instead of the idealized version of me he held; that I hoped this sweater would keep him warm.

I remembered the former boyfriend, who'd taken me to the prom and shared his passion for music with me—all his dreams and potential had ended so horribly.

Sometimes, I found myself crying.

Learning the Joy

The year moved into the depths of winter and the dampness grew even more intense, though I could have sworn such a thing would have been physically impossible. Auntie Peggy and

I took hot-water bottles to bed with us at night, and during the day, I knitted sweaters for my friends back home as Christmas gifts. A black short-sleeve boatneck for Sherri, who'd stayed with me through the boyfriend's death. A blue-and-purple mohair vest for Kathleen, who'd sung a heart-wrenching version of "Ave Marie" at my mother's funeral. The physical therapy was working and I could walk better now; I was healing. With knitting needles in hand, I was making peace with the coldness that encircled me and allowing the ache in my chest to become an acknowledged companion. I knit and purled, sat still and breathed, metaphorically weaving the disparate parts of myself back into a cohesive whole.

When it came time to say good-bye to Aunt Peggy, my cousins, and the foreign homeland that had allowed me temporary shelter in its damp greenness, I had more than sweaters to bring back. I had a sense of who I was, and though the wounds of loss weren't fully healed, I was making progress. I had glimpsed the wood at my core and had come to appreciate the simple grain found there. I had a new confidence that I could undertake a long, detailed project and actually stick with it— something I'd never done before—and many more gifts I wouldn't come to recognize until years later.

Using the Craft

Back home, I knit while studying at the university library. I knit in classes when I could get away with it. At my first job, doing public relations for a hospital and reporting to the media on the medical status of drive-by shooting victims, I knit as an escape from what I'd witnessed in the Emergency Room.

Today, as a professional writer, knitting is one of my best tools. Often, I get stuck on a transition, a plot point, or a question of character development. If I just keep hammering at the work, I usually make a mess of things, and sitting down to "think it over" is too focused—I get nowhere.

Ah, but knitting . . .

Something comforting, magical, and other-worldly happens when I knit. My hands tell me that I'm being active, that I'm not wasting time just staring out a window. I don't consciously think about the writing challenges I'm facing; rather, subterranean forces do what must be done to work out the issue. I don't always get answers. Usually, the real benefit is when I become centered enough to rephrase the question or to sit quietly with the not-knowing. The process doesn't always work as quickly as I'd like, but it always works.

Not long ago, when I decided I wanted to write a novel, I chided myself, afraid that I would never be able to keep at it. Novel-writing is a long, drawn-out process. Then a friend and fellow writer (who didn't know about my knitting obsession) shared with me a quote.

"Writing a novel is like knitting an argyle sock," she said, waiting a beat before continuing the analogy: "A sock the size of a football field." That quip, which was supposed to illustrate the complexity, size, and sheer lunacy of the undertaking—the craziness of thinking you can really do this—had the opposite effect on me.

I went to my cedar chest and pulled out the insanely difficult Fair Isle sweater I'd made the year before. In order to knit it, I'd had to teach myself to knit left-handed so that I could work two colors—one held in each hand—simultaneously. If I could do that, what was a football field-sized argyle sock to fear?

Since I've begun knitting, I've read books and articles, talked to psychologists and biofeedback specialists about the calming effect of this craft and the way it can induce trance states. I've attended lectures on related subjects, like spinning wool as spiritual practice, and found my idea—that knitting can be useful as a meditative/spiritual tool—is not as far out there as I'd anticipated. But even if all the experts didn't agree, I'd still know what knitting does for me. Knitting taps into my creative brain and uncovers untold treasures. In the sweaters I make for others, I gently pass on my positive desires for their lives; these garments give warmth while embracing the wearer in a hundred-thousand little prayers. And when I knit for myself, the resulting sweater is a tangible reminder that I can make my own warmth in what is often a cold world. When I knit, as when I write, I find myself in ecstatic participation in a divinely animated world.

I began knitting with modest hopes: a few minutes of communion with an elderly aunt, the chance to sit quietly for a moment in the midst of grief, and maybe even a raggedy sweater to show for it. I've gotten so much more.

 Try This

If you don't know how to knit, go to a local knitting shop and have the kind workers there teach you. Often, if you buy your supplies from the knitting shop, they'll throw in a lesson free. If you *do* know how to knit, take some time to teach someone else: a coworker, your best friend, your spouse, or a child (even boys like knitting). By doing so, you'll be giving a gift that may be greatly treasured and, for the most part, can only be learned in person. The best approach is one-on-one, with hands entwined, creating something together with someone you love.

chapter two

Feeding the Soul

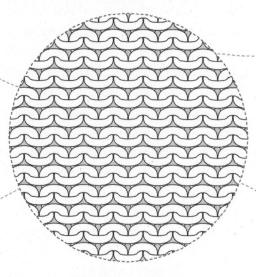

Garter Stitch

This stitch is made by knitting every row. A garter stitch makes a very stretchy kind of fabric. Should a firmer texture be desired, work into the back of each stitch.

The Rhythm of the Soul

My twelve-year-old son, Jarrod, plays trumpet in a jazz group, and I'm usually the one to take him to the rehearsals in downtown Los Angeles. Often, I bring a knitting project to work on during the two or three hours he's behind closed doors. A few other parents wait with me, though most drop their children off and return later. The kids work with their jazz teacher in an almost completely soundproof room. When a piece they're practicing becomes particularly loud, the slightest vibrations and melody slip through the soundproofing like smoke signals to let us know something wonderful is occurring in that little room. Hearing those sounds, I sneak up to the small five-by-ten-inch window and peer in.

I'm not the only one. Passersby, parents, people waiting for their dance classes to start: we all take turns jostling to watch preteen kids blow inspired, improvised jazz and blues. There's something irresistible about watching people do something they love.

The rehearsals take place in a gorgeous performing arts school situated next to the Museum of Contemporary Art (MOCA), a stone's throw from the Music Center's Dorothy Chandler Pavilion and in the shadow of the still-under-construction Disney Concert Hall, which is being raised up at astounding angles, huge sails of metal and concrete reminding Angelenos of imagination's incredible power. The school is located in an area that's both highly cultured and adjacent to great poverty; skid row is a few blocks away. It's a place where art, music, and dance—self-expression of all forms—are actively encouraged and yet the implicit risk in such self-expression is tangibly present. The unspoken fear, at least among the adults, seems to be: If I give myself so fully to something I love, will I end up like that street-corner poet I passed while looking for a parking space? The woman was screeching her words at approaching vehicles, trying to call attention to her beliefs and experiences, only to be drowned out by the forward-marching parade of society. Or what about the homeless man outside MOCA, strumming his guitar, happy in his music yet oblivious to the rest of the world: Will I become like him?

One of the biggest dangers of giving in to art is that our values might change—or return to an earlier, simpler form. The perfect house, the right furniture, the great job, the hip clothes: Maybe those things don't represent our hearts' desires the way we thought. Maybe we'll learn something about ourselves that we didn't particularly want to know. Or maybe people will laugh at us. Maybe we won't appear the way we'd like to appear.

Worse yet: Maybe we won't be any good at what we love.

And yet, those who indulge their talents so lavishly attract us all. It's one of the reasons our society is obsessed with celebrities. We're drawn to the energy produced by talent, by concentration, by hard work in the face of uncompromising odds. As I sit outside the jazz rehearsal room listening to the cadence of the tap dancers next door meld with the bleats of saxophones and the quiver of piano chords, I can't help thinking there's something wonderfully old-fashioned about people who will spend hours upon hours practicing a particularly difficult shuffle-step or learning to play a scale pocked with sharps or flats, bringing to life musical transcription that pre-dates the city. This hard work, dedication to craft, and willing-ness to persevere as the learning curve gains intensity is undeniably attractive. Maybe that's in part because such quali-ties are rare these days.

Today, we can play basketball on a video monitor and experience all the satisfaction of scoring without ever holding a tangible basketball in our hands and feeling its heft, without having to try and fail and try and fail, and without ever feeling our shoulders grow sore from the effort and our feet hot from pounding the pavement. Who wouldn't choose Nintendo over the asphalt court outside? No need to get sweaty and dirty. Similar satisfactions are available to all of us in digital formats. Music is a flip of a switch away—on television, the radio, and CDs—and dance has become yet another way to sell us prod-ucts. Why read good books when Hollywood will give you an easy-to-swallow film adaptation? By the same token, why take the time and energy to knit a sweater when you can buy five factory-produced ones instead? Why put yourself through the paces of creation, all that work? The celebrities in our culture are there to save you from that effort, the media tell us, to save you from the fear of embarrassment, the hassle, the grind.

Unfortunately, they also save us from exploring ourselves, from finding the talents that are lurking within, just waiting for a chance, and from finding the unspeakable joy in creating some-thing with our own hands, minds, bodies.

Next door to the jazz room is the tap dancing studio. When the tap dancers get going, everyone in that part of the building is drawn to the long landscape window that overlooks the scuffed-wood floor. Shouldered together, we, the impromptu audience, become mesmerized by the beat of the dancer's feet, the thrumming of the music, the synchronized movement of the students. Like a flock of birds turning all at once or the symmetry of waves pulled upon the shore, their motion entrances and calls for attention. For the first time that day, perhaps, we become aware of our own heartbeat. Our feet start moving just a toe at a time, our hands beat out a corresponding rhythm on our thighs. Something calls us to join in. And yet we usually content ourselves to watch, feeling a vague happiness at seeing others so fully exploring themselves. Dancers arc and curl and move in perfect coherence, as the rest of us, spectators at this celebration of life, watch for five or ten minutes before moving on, usually mumbling as we go, "I wish I could do that."

I look from the studio to the stitches in my hand. When I'm waiting outside the jazz room and knitting, invariably one of the other parents—usually a mother—will check out the project I'm working on, comment on how lovely it is, and tell me how she's never been able to knit. She might share a story about being taught in home economics class in seventh grade, but explain how she never got the hang of it. The conversation, regardless of the person making the comment, usually ends on the same note: "I wish I could do that."

Over the countless weeks I've been ensconced in the halls of this performing arts school, amazing things have begun to happen—or maybe they've been happening all along and I'm only just now noticing. A few of the parents who've watched the tap dancers have recently signed up for tap dancing lessons themselves. They've embraced an important truth: You don't have to be a kid to enjoy dancing. Or as the novelist Tom Robbins put it: "It's never too late to have a happy childhood." Even those adults who are older and have two left feet realize they can get out there on that very same floor that the professionals-in-training use; they can have a go at it. They won't look as coordinated as those incredibly talented youngsters, but who cares? It's their life. The beat is calling. Their feet are tapping. The smile of childhood splits the tension in their face. The time is now. Dance.

Children who've watched me knit often ask if I'll teach them how. Children seem less afraid to try something new than most adults, but that may be changing as well. Adults have begun asking, have become willing to take the risk. Maybe we've grown tired of letting television stars have all the fun.

Ironically, though, the recent interest among young women can be traced to the increasing numbers of knitting celebrities. If Winona Ryder, Julia Roberts, and Hilary Swank like it, the thinking seems to go, maybe I will, too. There've been blurbs in *People* magazine recently about Julianne Moore, Daryl Hannah, and other needle-wielding celebrities, demonstrating to readers just how hip knitting has become.

But I think the trend goes deeper than simple celebrity imitation. My theory is that we've grown so tired of looking and dressing and thinking the same—buying our coffee at Starbucks and wearing our Gap khakis, cutting our hair like Jennifer Aniston or Winona Ryder and going out to the multiplexes to see the same movies—that we're hungering for some way to show our originality.

In a quieter way than the performing arts, perhaps, knitting is attractive and soul-feeding. It's original. Its focus is to create something one-of-a-kind. If you ever knit in public, you'll see that many people stop to stare. People ask questions, initiate conversation, follow your movements. Some sit down just to hear the clack, clack, clack of the needles and be lulled by the physical rhythm of your hands.

※

My son's jazz group will give their first performance of the semester this afternoon, making music on the same stage where such luminaries as Wynton Marsalis and the Los Angeles Chamber Orchestra have performed. Everyone in the family has dressed up, and we've invited the in-laws and some friends to come along. I sit in the concert hall noticing the near-perfect acoustics of the room, feeling a fluttery anxiousness. The seats are sparsely filled. The flyer that had been sent out to announce the concert listed no specific time, though I'm not sure if that omission is solely to blame for the low turnout. The intimate hall is less than a quarter occupied. How sad, I think, that this first concert is such a nonevent.

The lights dim, the kids come on stage looking small and timid, but the music they create is beyond wonderful. I look around at the in-laws and friends we've brought along. They're enjoying the music, but clearly they're not seeing and hearing what I am. They see and hear a handful of kids blow some nice tunes through a heavy veil of shyness, kids who are working together in a kind of stilted harmony, making accomplished music but looking throughout like the awkward ingenuous children they are.

I see in their performance all the moments that have led to it. The hours of practice instead of TV time or video games. The moment my son decided to drop the football team because it was interfering with his music. The rehearsals the kids themselves organized (sometimes I sat in)—six twelve-year-olds crammed into a tiny practice room. They'd figure out how'd they'd perform a given piece—who'd solo first, how they'd come back to the melody, who'd set the tempo, how they'd end. The first time Jarrod soloed with this group of kids, they encouraged him, egged him on. I witnessed the recognition click that day when he realized he could make his own music—not just the music he could read, but the music he could imagine. Miles Davis once said that his job wasn't to read the notes that were printed on the page, but the notes that *weren't* on the page.

Sitting in the concert hall, I realize that they've already given the big performance. Over a series of days, stuck in the cramped rehearsal room, a baseball cap sitting backwards on my son's head: Those were the important times. Today's performance with everyone all dressed up is no more than a formality, a confirmation of what has already occurred.

What I've come to know about knitting and writing and most everything else that matters a great deal to me applies as well to my son's music. I look at sweaters I've made and I don't see a garment; I see the tough time I had figuring the neck out. The way the multicolored ribbing drove me to distraction trying to understand how to make it work. The way I unwound the hanks of wool when they first arrived, feeling the lanolin and drinking in the colors, imagining what the finished sweater would look like. Once the sweater was done, though, the process was over. Sometimes, the finished product didn't live up to my expectations, just as today's jazz performance—the lack of attendance, the unimpressed nature of the audience—didn't live up. Few things in life ever satisfy our expectations. And yet, in other ways, my pleasure goes so far beyond my expectations: learning a new stitch; discovering a different manner of reducing for shoulders; creating an alternate way of piecing a sweater together. Those were the real moments. And in doing so, I have created something beautiful, something original—a piece of wearable art that has never existed before.

When I hold a finished sweater in my hand, I hold tangible proof that I know more than I think I do and that I'm intelligent. As my dear friend Nancy—who, as a single mother of four girls, went back to college, made it through medical school, and is now a family practice physician—used to remind me: Intelligence isn't having all the answers. Intelligence is the capacity to learn what you don't know. The sweaters I knit remind me of this. They remind me that life is too short to stand outside the window of the tap dancing studio saying, I wish I could do that.

Be Still and Know That I Am God

It's April in Southern California. I'm sitting on my front porch
on a warm, mid-eighties morning watching newly hatched butterflies. The air is thick with them. They make shadows across
the pad of paper on my lap. I write for a bit. I knit for a bit.
People walk past. Corporate workers with cell phones attached
to belts, work shoes temporarily replaced by sneakers, are out
for a brisk morning walk, a break from the hustling business district three blocks over. The Armenian produce vendor pulls up
in a battered van and honks his horn for the grandmothers in
the neighborhood to come out and buy fresh basil, fruit, and
lettuce—the farmer's market goods he sells street by street.
Urban moms in hipster clothes slink by pushing fat-faced babies
in jogging strollers. A mockingbird darts overhead, perches, and
begins to sing. The scent of flowers from the tree in front of the
house is heavy, like too much Chanel in too small a bathroom.
Little buds from the arching limbs fall onto my hair, my knitting,
my writing. The fountain that sits next to me on the porch is
spitting water, strumming a rhythmic bass line for the riffs of
cars and trash trucks and approaching sirens. Everyone who
passes comments on the glorious day. I pick up my knitting,
watch a dog trot across my shabby lawn with his owner in tow,
and recognize what a charmed life I lead.

This city is a contradiction—urban, fast-paced, and con-
gested on one hand, alive with butterflies and birds, produce
men and Old World women, even yuppies who stop to say
hello, on the other. In a similar way, my self-image and my

knitting are a contradiction: I consider myself a feminist and an aspiring intellectual, a woman of the twenty-first century; yet I sit on a rickety beach chair on an old Craftsman porch in the middle of a busy city on a beautiful spring day, knitting. I am a working writer and a stay-at-home mom simultaneously. I advocate for women's rights, craft fictional stories and factual essays, and knit beautiful pieces of handiwork from the same source. Without having to dress up for church or temple, I see the hand of God in the details of my everyday existence. In my life, it all comes as a package.

Spirituality has always interested me, and though I haven't found the concrete answers I'd initially hoped to find in my search for an understanding of God, I've learned something altogether different and maybe more precious: I've learned to make peace with the chaotic nature of life, to sit still when upheaval surrounds me, to do nothing when nothing is required. I'm not a specialist in Buddhism nor an expert on Zen. I've studied world religions, I've soaked up as much as I could about different ways of looking into spiritual conundrums, I've meditated, and I've prayed. The insights I've gained into the spiritual and creative benefits of knitting seem Zen-like to me in their emphasis on finding the holy spark in everyday life, in sitting still, in letting things unfold.

Sometimes walking my children to school in the morning, going over their spelling words, and talking with them about the day ahead is the most spiritual moment of my day. Other times, after I've seen them to their classes, I take a slow stroll home, alone amid the rumble of the city and commuters on their streaking way. These are the moments that the God of my understanding is manifest in my life. Not to say that God, or however you might refer to the creative life force, isn't always there. But it is in those moments when I make a conscious effort to be fully awake to the beauty of my life that I most keenly notice God's presence gracing the scene.

For me, this is what knitting does. I stop to see the precise color of the sky, to hear the bird's song and look amid the tree branches for the song's source. Right now, sitting on my porch, I smell the exact fragrance of the blossoms that fall on my head, a fragrance warmed by the sun on this day, cooled on others to a barely detectable scent. To be here, right now in this moment: That is the reason I knit.

I have always been an intellectual person, convinced that smart thinking could achieve the things I wanted. It's taken a simple ball of wool and two pointy sticks to show me another way. Operating within my hands, these tools demonstrate the richness of life beyond my own limited intellect. Knitting reminds me that I'm like the yarn I knit. The substance of me—carbon, water, organic matter—has been in existence for eons, way before the specific incarnation of me drew my first breath. Like a ball of wool waiting to be transformed into a sweater, I existed in some form long before I existed. Now that I am animate, my actions, my words, my knitting, my aesthetics exist in a real and tangible way. But just as a sweater can be pulled apart and unraveled, returned to the earlier ball of wool, so too will the elements I am composed of return to dust, the particles of me rejoining the earth. In the meantime, the pattern and construction of my life, as well as of the sweater I'm knitting, are in my hands. I may look to the designs others have used as inspiration. I may change plans midstream. I might follow a pattern exactly as written or create my own unique statement. But in the end, I am the one who makes these stitches with my actions, my words, my thoughts. I construct the pattern of my life in the same way I construct a sweater. Piece by piece, stitch by stitch.

Knitting is a metaphor for so many things in life. I can't help thinking this way. As a writer, almost everything I see becomes a metaphor on some level. Yet, few things lend themselves so easily, so wisely to a metaphorical understanding of life as does knitting. Think about it for a moment. Knitting is ancient and connects us with all the knitters who've come before us. Knitting tells me that just as a sweater is made up of countless stitches, countless sections that of themselves seem rather meaningless, so my life is made up of the many countless actions I take. Every kind word or cutting remark, the moments when I recognize the wonder of life and the many times I fail to do so, all these seemingly inconsequential moments add up, stitch upon stitch, to create the fabric of my life.

There is one crucial aspect, though, in which knitting is most dissimilar from life: With knitting, we have the ability to undo what we've done and correct mistakes, leaving no sign of what had previously been wrong. In knitting as in life, mistakes multiply. If you make too many increases for a sleeve, say, and continue without correcting the problem, you will eventually distort the shape of that sleeve. My own actions may have similar repercussions. A hurtful word or a painful memory may continue to distort the shape of my life. When this occurs, I need to go back and identify the place where things went wrong and then do my utmost to correct them.

The difficult truth, though, is that there are no "do-overs" in life. We can make amends, but we can't erase what has been done.

The ability to go back and correct mistakes in knitting also teaches me about perfectionism. Sometimes it's worth ripping out stitches and redoing whole sections of a project, spending hours or days fixing an error that will forever mar the garment. Other mistakes, though, can be accepted. There are times when good enough is just that. With knitting, as in daily life, I'm learning to embrace the spirituality of imperfection. A friend recently told me of an afghan his grandmother had knit. "See this," she'd said to him, pointing out a section that had an error. "We are human," she told him. "Perfection is beyond us."

Knitting, it seems to me, also provides a new understanding of linear time. The act of knitting requires an accretion of countless moments, and in a sense the knitted piece contains them all. Just as a photograph will ricochet me back to the moment it was snapped, touching a sweater I've knit makes the moments of its creation blossom again in a visceral, fully imagined way. In some sense the time spent knitting that sweater is gone forever, and yet, it's still completely accessible to me via the sweater. The time I've spent knitting is less elusive than most of life's moments—when I'm rushing through, getting the job done, meeting the deadline, making the dinner, when I'm focused on the completion of some task and fail to see the moment fully.

I'm reminded of Thornton Wilder's play, *Our Town,* about the girl Emily who dies as a young woman. She's given the chance to come back to relive part of her life and is appalled by how casually everyone takes the precious gifts of life and of family love. She tries to get her mother to see the miracle of existence that's before her, but her mother has food to prepare and busywork to do. "But, just for a moment now we're all together," Emily says to her mother, trying to show her what a blessing this one day is. "Mama, just for a moment we're happy." Emily, reduced to tears, begs her mother, Mama, please, *"Let's look at one another."*

When I knit, I stop to look. I take the time to be still and know that God is God. I find in those moments the peace of mind necessary to see clearly the miracle of my own existence, the preciousness of those I love. I get a glimpse once again of the goodness found in daily life and the many, many ways my life is graced.

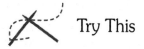 Try This

Make a scarf for yourself or someone you love. A very simple pattern is to cast on 30 stitches with a bulky wool on size 10 needles. Knit the first row. Do a 2 × 2 rib on the second row (knit 2, purl 2). Repeat these two rows until desired length or until you run out of wool. The scarf will curl in towards itself in a cozy way. For a variation, change yarn colors as you go (orange and lime, or whatever color combination gets you going—you can even use up your leftover wool, changing colors whenever the skeins end). This prismatic scarf will add brightness to the dreariest day and remind loved ones of the colors they add to your life.

chapter three

Resting the Mind

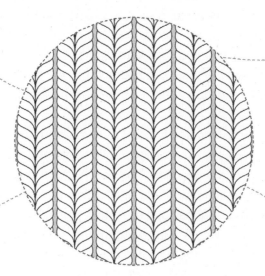

Stockinette Stitch
(also known as Jersey)

This stitch is the most common found in knitting. It makes a distinctive pattern of Vs across the right side. Note that the ends of the knitted areas will curl unless there's a ribbing or some other evening-out stitch at the ends. If you like the rolled look, use this stitch without ribbing.

Row 1: knit all the way across
Row 2: purl all the way across
Repeat rows 1 and 2 to desired length.

This Is Your Brain.
This Is Your Brain on Knitting.

There's been a lot written in recent years on the benefits of meditation and what, exactly, constitutes meditative practice. Some have speculated that knitting could be a true form of meditation, similar in custom and result to the meditative practice found in Zen Buddhism. I researched this topic to see what I might uncover.

In the more traditional forms of meditation, those typically associated with Eastern religions, meditation has been defined as a state of "bare attention." As Ron Nairn puts it in *What Is Meditation?*, meditation is "a highly alert and skillful state of mind because it requires one to remain psychologically present and 'with' whatever is happening in and around one without adding to or subtracting from it in any way."

According to an article in *Psychology Today* on psychology and meditation, the physical act of meditation can consist of sitting quietly and focusing on your breath, a word, or a phrase; the meditator may also be walking or standing.

The image we all carry of a person tied into lotus-position knots, sitting in a candlelit, incense-choked room, hands held upward, saying "ohm" in a low, sonorous voice may be a limited construct. There are countless ways, it seems, to practice meditation.

Researchers agree that the practice of meditation has untold health benefits—improvements that can be gleaned from as little as ten minutes of meditation on a regular basis. These benefits include increased alpha waves (the relaxed brain waves) and decreased anxiety and depression. Researchers at Harvard Medical School used MRI technology to monitor participants' brain activity and learned that meditation activates the portion of the brain responsible for the autonomic nervous system (the regulator of bodily functions outside our conscious control) including digestion and blood pressure "These are also the functions that are often compromised by stress," a writer on the subject, Cary Barbor, reported in *Psychology Today.* "It makes sense, then, that modulating these functions would help to ward off stress-related conditions such as heart disease, digestive problems, and infertility."

A number of studies have shown benefits of meditation. One such study showed that meditation helps reverse heart disease, that it reduces pain, and enhances one's immune system, enabling it to better fight disease. With a group of cancer patients who were taught to meditate, for instance, a different study showed that meditation increases energy while reducing depression, anxiety, anger, confusion, and heart and gastrointestinal problems.

The definition of meditative practice has grown, too. Scientists such as Herbert Benson, M.D., the founding president of the Mind/Body Medical Institute at the Harvard Medical School, now believe that a range of meditative practices, including knitting, can elicit the "relaxation response" (the beneficial changes in brain physiology engendered by meditation). According to Benson, there are two basic steps necessary to evoke this relaxation response, steps that he found to be present in almost every culture around the globe. The first is the repetition of a sound, phrase, or prayer. (This, by extension, includes the repetition of an activity, like making a knitted stitch.) The second step is the passive setting aside of intruding thoughts and returning to the repetition.

Benson writes in *Psychology Today* that "through the simple act of changing their thought patterns, the subjects experienced decreases in their metabolism, breathing rate, and brain wave frequency. These changes appeared to be the opposite of the commonly known 'fight-or-flight' response and I called it the 'relaxation response.'" If practiced daily, this relaxation response can boost the immune system and make it more resistant to the harmful effects of constant stress.

I spoke with one of Dr. Benson's colleagues, Peg Baim, the clinical director for training at the Mind/Body Institute at Harvard. Even among the young, she said, intense stress "alters brain physiology" and is implicated in many illnesses. "If you have a genetic propensity for a certain disease and are under a lot of stress, the system of checks and balances designed to keep you well goes kablooey—it's ruined unless you counter the stress."

Most knitters know this already. Knitter after knitter related stories of how the handcraft had a calming, soothing effect on his or her life. But the fact that the medical establishment is beginning to see the link and how it impacts physical well-being as well as mental health may be news. I asked Peg whether knitting is *always* a meditative experience. I've taught people to knit and have seen their shoulders bunched up around their ears, their hands almost in knots, trying to do what I was showing them. I'd be hard-pressed to consider that experience "meditative."

Peg assured me that, no, knitting in and of itself is not necessarily a form of meditation.

"I know people who can turn knitting into something harmful for them," she said. "It's all on how you approach it." To illustrate the mindfulness and attention one needs while knitting to engender the relaxation response, Peg said to think of a neurosurgeon "who's quite relaxed while doing very difficult, highly concentrated work." Knitters must have a similar attitude. Peg told me of a brilliant researcher who's looking into questions of "flow," which might be another way of eliciting the relaxation response. "The key," she said, "is to stay in a state of openness and to bring to your work an attitude of interest. Stay out of your judging mind."

Often, self-criticism can stand in the new knitter's way. The sense of relaxation and meditation won't be forthcoming as long as you're worried about doing it wrong or making a mistake.

Newness, though, is not the only stumbling block to finding nirvana. "I know older, long-term knitters who drive themselves nuts," Peg said. "But they drive themselves nuts no matter what they're doing, perfectionism being one of the big ways."

When people meditate or participate in a meditative activity like knitting, Peg said, they increase their creativity, shut off their spatial awareness and time orientation, and they may experience oneness, unity, expansion, feelings of hope, and awe. These "spiritual" experiences are a part of our brain's physiology. "You also increase your concentration," said Peg.

"Most anything can be meditative," Peg explained, "including a stroll through a museum." If you look at the art with an openness to levels of interpretation, "not judging but taking the art in as beauty, inspiration, insight, being pinned to your interest, using your child's mind," you can trigger the same relaxation response.

To get the most out of your knitting time, then, Peg suggested that you have an intended focus and an attitude of interest. For example, say you're working on a sweater for a newborn baby. The attitude of interest could be an openness towards the process of making the sweater, a willingness to follow all the steps necessary, and a lack of impatience to get to the end. The intended focus would be the newborn baby or the mother towards whom you are expressing love by your behavior of knitting. This frame of mind can put one into a state of deep, contemplative meditation. The Mind/Body Medical Institute teaches patients concentration strategies necessary for such contemplation. But just by knitting, Peg said, "We learn those same concentration strategies."

OK. So we know we relax when we knit. Beyond relaxation, though, what else happens? It's always seemed to me that something more essential than just relaxation is occurring. Does the brain physiology show anything else? I asked.

Creativity happens, Peg told me, along with a sense of transcending the self.

If we look into the brain physiology, we'll see that the area of the brain that is usually activated by creativity is also activated by meditation. "If it's activated a lot, has a lot of activity, it's producing more signals, processing more input, turning on that part of the brain." Thus, the great "high" I get in creating anything—an inspired vegetable soup, say, or an insightful paragraph—is the same euphoria I feel from knitting. Not just the finished garment, but the entire process: *I'm making something. Me. These hands with this yarn and this series of movements is making something!*

Knitting keeps my creativity muscles working. As with a physical muscle in the body, atrophy sets in if I don't use my creativity for some time. When I try to do something inspired after a long hiatus from my own imagination, I find I'm rusty. I'm hesitant. But when I keep honoring and responding to my artistic self, my stores of creativity continue to grow and flourish, the muscles of my imagination become stronger.

At the same time that I'm lighting up the creativity center in my brain, Peg told me, I'm also shutting off other parts of the brain, particularly the temporal lobe (that part of the brain that causes us to feel separate and that handles time and space orientation). "There's no activity there at all," Peg explained.

An article in *Newsweek*, which looked into the neurological underpinnings of spiritual and mystical experiences, reported similar findings. Scientists have used a special type of brain imaging (SPECT) to snap a photo of the transcendent experience. "As expected, the prefrontal cortex, the seat of attention, lit up" during meditation. Meanwhile, "A bundle of neurons in the superior parietal lobe, toward the top and back of the brain, had gone dark." This region, also known as the "orientation association area," is the part of the brain that processes information about time and space, as well as the orientation of one's body in space.

Some consider this occurrence a form of "temporal lobe seizure" in which you lose your sense of ego boundaries. Peg said: "We can extrapolate that in meditation and prayer, and yes, even knitting, one experiences a sense of timelessness and an expansion beyond ego boundaries." Meditation prevents the brain from forming the distinction between yourself and others. "The meditators feel that they have touched infinity," *Newsweek* reported. All sense of separateness and aloneness disappear, replaced instead with feelings of unity, of timelessness, of eternity. This accounts for the spiritual aspects engendered by any form of meditation, including knitting. But does this mean one accesses nirvana or God during knitting? Not necessarily.

No one knows whether these feelings are just neurological firings that occur in human brains for some inexplicable reason—a light show of our own making—or whether they confirm a spiritual reality that we recognize on some deeper, subconscious level. It's possible that this awareness reflects an underlying unity, a connectedness between every form of life that hasn't yet been confirmed by science—that we are all of a piece. Still, at this time, the evidence is inconclusive. "[T]here is no way to determine whether the neurological changes . . . mean that the brain is causing those experiences . . . or is instead perceiving a spiritual reality," said the article in *Newsweek*.

For myself, at least, it doesn't necessarily matter what exactly causes me to feel relaxed, connected, and at peace. Whether I am tapping into a spiritual reality beyond the reckoning of my logical mind or I am simply responding to neurological impulses, I'm happy to reap the benefits.

As Peg put it, "Creativity, spirituality, and meditation are all linked." Many people think of them as being separate from each other, distinct entities; but brain physiology ties them all together.

So That's What I'm Doing

Marie Blauvelt of Great Barrington, Massachusetts, is a forty-two-year-old knitter who makes her living as a medical receptionist. She learned to knit in the early eighties when she worked in publishing and her company decided to launch a line of knitting books. The president of the company taught Marie to knit using *Vogue* magazine as her only resource. For Marie, the knitting "began to fill a creative urge that I never knew I had, as well as a mental challenge—learning a completely different language, so to speak. I began as a technical 'nerd' and couldn't get enough reading material to keep me satisfied. It was also a way for me to express this endless, bottomless love I felt for my new daughter."

Knitting soon became as much a part of her daily life as brushing her teeth. "When I am emotionally in need of centering, my knitting is the quickest, cheapest, most familiar way for me to do that."

But is it a genuine form of meditation?

To answer, Marie told the story of her relationship with her best friend, who was hooked into a variety of new age resources. "He would often treat me to weekend meditation retreats, buy me books and tapes, send me lovely things like oils, crystals, and so on." Marie's reaction, though, left something to be desired. Clearly, he wanted her to encounter some of the benefits he'd gleaned from his own meditative practice, but it wasn't happening for Marie. "These gifts did not achieve the 'transporting' quality he wanted me to experience," she said.

Everything changed when she brought her knitting to a silent meditation retreat they attended. Her body language and facial expression while she was knitting and the thoughts and inspirations they shared afterwards told them both that she'd already received via knitting what he'd been trying to give her as a gift. They laughed when they recognized that he could have saved all that money and guided her to achieve altered states by "just put my knitting in my hands."

Marie said that when she knits, her eyes soften, as if her senses are working, but she's not really in the room. "It is a thorough getaway for me. I can function, listen, and see, but from a remove." Her muscles loosen, and the mind orders and sorts itself. She quoted a friend in France who lost a child, saying she knits "pour vider la tete"—to empty the head.

From this activity, Marie has learned patience, fortitude, and the art of sticking with something to see it through. She's also learned that because it is a "sanctioned" activity, you can do it anywhere and not have to brook disapproving frowns. Knitting seems to be universally viewed, in her experience, as industrious and worthwhile.

On a metaphysical level, Marie said that when she knits for someone she loves, she thinks of that person continually throughout the project and knows that "there is an intangible quality to the finished garment that the person will some-how 'feel.'"

For her, knitting is a positive statement, a trust and belief in tomorrow. "When I suffered from a bout of depression several years ago, I had trouble picking up the knitting. Once my out-look was restored, it greeted me like a lost friend." Knitting helped Marie rediscover her internal peace. Also, she said, it's still the best way for her to travel, literally as well as meta-physically. "It can either pull me out of an unpleasant environ-ment or keep me pleasantly occupied and in heightened awareness within it."

Currently, Marie's favorite knitting project is making socks. "They have always been the thing I reach for when I'm at loose ends, knitting-wise or otherwise. They are comforting, practical, and still a mystery to me in some respects. I also like thinking that I'm taking the trouble to make something that is going to be concealed inside a shoe—kind of gives you an inner smile, if that makes sense."

Socks seem to be a favorite of many contemplative knitters, including Alexandra Grant, known as Xan, who lives in Austin, Texas. She appreciates socks because "they finish fast and wear well and are great gifts." Xan has retired from her work as a fundraiser for PBS, a job she held for fifteen years. In my interviews with her, Xan offered a wonderful, mystical account of her knitting process, providing me with generous e-mails and prose poems about the joy of knitting.

Xan learned to knit when she was ten years old, sitting on a front porch in Montgomery, Alabama, teaching herself from a book. She abandoned the craft when the teen years set in, only to pick it up again with her first pregnancy. Like many knitters I interviewed, Xan got snarled up working with acrylic yarns, disliking the feel of them and yet unaware of resources for natural fibers. She never finished the early acrylic baby sweater, though she did knit "a gross brown thing" for herself before putting the needles down for many years. In the 1970s, living on a commune in California, she began to crochet, making skirts and "colorful stuff," entertaining "fantasies of packing around the globe with a bag full of yarn, creating and selling from place to place."

It wasn't until 1980, when she was living in San Francisco and happened upon the wonderful yarn shops in the Bay Area, that she rediscovered knitting. "From then on," she wrote, knitting became "something more," a "continuous discovery." She bought a *Vogue Knitting* book, trudged many tomes from the library, switched from flat knitting to using circular needles exclusively, and began to design, seeing everything around her as knitting patterns: Landscapes. Skyscapes. Innerscapes. She used smaller and smaller needle sizes, between 0 and 3, and learned to discern fibers that fit with Texas, where she had since settled. Wool doesn't work well in Texas, she explained, and lighter choices require wholly different techniques.

Xan says she often knits for other people, but doesn't necessarily know what she's making when she begins. "I'm knitting simply because there is something I want to make. I discover for whom or what as it develops."

"Knitting uses me in its necessary meditation," Xan explained. "Focus. Pattern. Habit. Intent. Making a garment; growing a life." She said that "following a process . . . allows the process itself to become the habit, a cloak of intent that takes one completely into one's isolated self, if we're lucky and practice well."

To more fully explain, she quoted Thich Nhat Hanh's book, *Living Buddha, Living Christ:*

Mindfulness is the key. When you become aware of something you begin to have enlightenment. When you drink from a glass of water and are aware that you are drinking from a glass of water deeply with your whole being, enlightenment is there in its initial form. To be enlightened about the fact that I am drinking a glass of water. I can obtain joy, peace, and happiness just because of that enlightenment . . . the substance of a Buddha is mindfulness . . . you only need to dwell deeply in the present moment.

"So I knit a glass of water," Xan said. "It is total prayer. It has always amazed me that one can take a thread of yarn and a couple of needles and make that into almost anything you want. To make a wearable garment, with all the energy, thought, subconscious meditations, and so on that occur as your hands manipulate the thread and the thread grows and grows into cloth—this is indeed 'growing a life.'"

Though Xan has thought from time to time about knitting for money and briefly worked in a yarn shop, for her, finishing other people's projects or knitting-to-order isn't much fun. She finds joy in her own creations. When she was a working woman, she knit in airports and at meetings and events whenever she could and then wore her own creations. That process "endowed me with the totality of knitting as art," which, she explained, is a form of "humbling happiness." She continued: "Wearing your own work invariably attracts notice. 'You MADE that! Look everyone, she MADE that!'"

Xan finds her part in keeping alive a very real art form humbling. "Working thread into cloth has to be among the oldest crafts, and it is certainly a part of myths and folktales and fairy tales from all parts of the world and ages. There is mystery and magic involved, and power—the power of the spider whose silken thread can both carry and capture." Craft is transforming matter.

In addition to a knitter, Xan is a poet and aspiring novelist, a sculptor, gardener, and cook. "Knitting is truly a boon, a space for subconsciously working through much matter," she said of her other creative ventures. In thinking about the ways knitting has impacted her life, Xan sent me a prose poem she'd written comparing knitting to "an adventure," with regular patterns like a dance, the fibers holding the memory of the weaver, and every finger and thread worker mystically held together by the stitches. She celebrated mistakes that bring "order to chaos to order to chaos again and again."

No Connection Between the Two

Though the idea of knitting as meditation has seemed self-evident to me, some knitters don't see it that way at all. For them, knitting is a craft, a hobby, not much more. Still, in their stories are traces of the meditative experience.

Take Cecile Bewley Toth, a medical transcriptionist in Lawson, Missouri, who said she doesn't use knitting as a tool for meditation or prayer. She has noted, however, that "my dog relaxes a lot when I am knitting. He sees what I am doing, knows that nothing in particular will be happening for a while, and just sleeps at my feet. He does this wherever we are: at home, in the car, even at dog shows." Though Cecile doesn't view her handcraft as anything particularly spiritual, still, she said she has gained great wisdom from the practice. "Steadiness is important," she wrote. "Just being steady about one thing when the rest of your life is in chaos can keep it all in balance." For her, the joy of knitting is to be found in the planning stages and then the creation of the finished work, more so than the actual finished garment. "I love to wear the garments, but they are just clothes. The planning and the process are far more important." Cecile prefers to work with textures and complex patterns, although doing a great deal of color work doesn't interest her. The process of knitting, for Cecile, is undoubtedly artistic. "I like the fact that something with terrific textures, cables, and pattern definition is almost like sculpting," she said. "Not only are you creating the fabric, but you are sculpting it as you go."

Kathy Montgolf, a full-time mother and part-time antique restorationist, remarked that her favorite kind of knitting project is "one I finish." Though she had little to say about meditation or relaxation as a result of her knitting, she said that she often uses her knitting time to ponder solutions for her antique restoration business. "I have, on occasion, figured out how to repair someone's antique," she said, "by letting it mull around in my head when I knit."

Perhaps the difference is just a matter of semantics. What I call meditative, another calls artistic or a form of trouble-shooting. Still, every knitter seems drawn to the craft in a deeply intuitive way.

Knitting as Therapy

I wondered about the mental health benefits of knitting. Having used knitting to calm my own often-turbulent mind, to center myself, and to regain emotional balance, I knew I couldn't be the only one. I contacted knitting psychologists to get their opinions.

Georgia Howorth Fair is a licensed marriage and family therapist in Orlando, Florida, who considers knitting to be her own personal form of therapy. So much of her work deals with emotional trauma and sexual and physical abuse, she explained. But knitting "is the antithesis of what I do in my work. It's calming and soothing. There's nothing traumatic about knitting."

For Georgia, many of the benefits of knitting are tied to her own mental well-being. "The benefit is in having a project I can actually finish. So much of my work is unfinished and changing; it seldom seems done. We're always moving to another level," she said of her work as a psychologist. Knitting, on the other hand, has a clear-cut beginning, middle, and end.

I asked Georgia about clients who knit, but she doesn't believe she has any. "Though everyone's talking about this resurgence in knitting," she said, "I'm not seeing it. Perhaps there are more famous people knitting and more people chatting on the Internet about knitting, but it seems that most people are so busy, they don't have time for it." This issue of time and busyness is indicative of larger problems in today's society and only reinforces our sense of isolation, she explained.

"The very busy people," Georgia said, "are looking for ways of distracting themselves, of not getting closer to themselves. Plus, knitting takes time, and they don't want to do anything that requires a time commitment. Also, you need someone to help you learn to knit, and we live in a time when people are very independent and don't want to need someone else or ask for help. We all go to work and do our jobs and maybe drive home alone and then go to our individual machines—computers, televisions, etc.—to distract ourselves from ourselves and each another. Knitting does the opposite, and maybe that frightens people off."

Georgia honors the need for community by going to her local knitting shop to participate in the Tuesday night knits. "It's a wonderful time to sit and talk and connect. In many respects, knitting is communal. Plus, for me, it's great to hear conversation that isn't traumatic and difficult. The stuff I hear all day long is the stuff people don't talk about in public. It's nice to talk about other things."

She lamented, though, that there are so few opportunities for this kind of social interaction in contemporary life. "That *was* our entertainment in times past, our way of being together," she said with a sudden vehemence in her voice. "In earlier days, people knew they couldn't survive without other people. Today, we think we can," she paused, "and that's what's so sad."

Georgia said she learned to knit when she was seven, taught by an older woman. "My father bought a rickety hotel and was going to turn it into a Hilton kind of thing," she explained. "The residents were old people who weren't well enough to live in a house on their own but who didn't yet need a nursing home. This lady had very arthritic hands and used knitting to help keep them nimble. She was very patient with me." The gift of knitting, given by that particular woman all those years ago, continues to bless Georgia's life. "The person who taught me was very special to have done so. There's not enough of that these days; not only people teaching each other, but the talk and the interaction. You don't just learn to knit. You share with that person and connect." The sense of loss was tangible in her voice.

Georgia was quick to warn newcomers, though, that learning to knit isn't like falling off a log.

"I have a friend who says she sweats when she knits," Georgia explained. "Like everything else, knitting has a learning curve. You benefit from each project you undertake."

As far as finding a spiritual or meditative outlet via knitting, Georgia was skeptical. "People have tried to draw parallels with meditation, and I'm not sure I buy them." The focusing she uses in knitting is *like* meditation, she explained. It's about pausing and getting quiet and centered. "But to me, it's more like eating a piece of pickled ginger after sushi to clear the palate." She has, however, experienced the immense joy of knitting for others. "A friend had asked me to knit chemo caps, but then a neighbor's sister was diagnosed with breast cancer and I made caps for her, though I never met her. It was a very moving experience. The caps were from a very soft chenille and she'd sleep in them. Her head hurt so much from the chemo and losing her hair and the little nubs of new hair growing in. She just loved them and it helped ease her pain." Her voice softened, taking in the expanse of her statement. "I don't know how to fully explain it except to say 'that was real.'"

Judith Parker, Ph.D., is a Los Angeles–based psychologist absolutely hooked on knitting. "It was just a progression as I got more and more fascinated with the creative possibilities in knitting: color, pattern, design, etc.," she explained. "As I got better at the techniques, I could get more creative and it became an expressive art, like a pianist who doesn't have to think about his or her fingers any longer but can just let the music express emotion."

Judith has seen a direct correlation between her own psychoanalytic treatment and the adeptness of her knitting. Her progress in psychoanalysis, sorting through and cleaning up the debris of her childhood, has cleared her mind. "As my mind has grown, I have watched my knitting improve tremendously, in that I can hold more in my mind, stay alert and undistracted for longer periods of time, and do more complex and challenging knitting projects with ease." She's confident that good psychoanalytic treatment improves the knitter's ability to concentrate and that the finished project reflects this improvement.

It's an interesting thought to consider.

Ask a handful of knitters what the most freeing experience of knitting has been for them, and you'll probably receive a handful of varied answers. For Judith, the freeing experience has been in knitting for other people and getting out of herself and her own expectations. When she's knitting for someone else, she's "not wondering or worrying about how a garment will look on *me*, but imagining how it will look on someone else." By shifting the focus to others, it seems, we become much less critical about our work.

Judith, like so many of the knitters I interviewed, said that the process, not the end result, was the ultimate satisfaction. This understanding made the hassle of ripping out stitching to correct errors much easier to embrace. "Un-knitting back to where one made a mistake," she said, "is just as valid a part of the process as knitting. Enjoy the ride."

Anna Walden is a psychologist located in San Diego, California, who started knitting in earnest after finishing her Ph.D., when she needed something new and nonacademic to engage in.

When she knits, she said she taps into another part of herself, a part without language that is emotional and creative. This break from language, Anna said, impacts her professional life as a psychologist where so much of her work is based in language. By doing something that takes her completely away from her work, she finds she can concentrate better when she *is* working. The experience of knitting centers her on the one hand and excites her on the other. "Knitting makes me a better person."

I asked how. "I'm not so one-sided, and the knitting has reduced the feelings of burnout." Anna is also grateful for the external pluses, especially for the courage and hope she's gleaned from other people who knit. "Being among knitters has made me braver about taking risks, improved my confidence, and that has carried over to other areas."

In recent years, Anna has made the leap from just knitting to designing. "I am now in business with two other women dying yarn and selling the designs." She credits Kaffe Fassett, whose playful use of color inspired her, with her transition from passive knitter to active designer. From the moment she discovered his color awareness, she realized that she could take classes and learn beyond what was in patterns and books. "I think breaking free of patterns and taking risks is another level of knitting," she explained, and a risk that is worth the angst involved in making the leap.

Knitters knit to meditate, to quiet themselves, to reach transcendence, to create art, to play with color, to appreciate texture, to strengthen their immune systems.

Mostly, knitters knit to be still.

Regardless of the reasons, there seems to be one unifying factor. Not a single knitter of those I interviewed said of her knitting time that she wished she were doing something else. Repeatedly, no matter how many people I asked, the same response was elicited: "When I'm knitting, there's nowhere else I'd rather be and nothing else I'd rather be doing."

To me, this sounds suspiciously like contentment, if not outright happiness. What a rare commodity these days! Interestingly, this came up in my conversation with Peg from the Mind/Body Health Institute at Harvard. Peg mentioned a researcher who's looking into the components of happiness, trying to define what combination of things are necessary to make people happy. She said that the researcher had found three connected elements that make for happiness. The first is to be involved in a creative endeavor, towards which you have an attitude of interest—you're absorbed by whatever it is you're making. The second component is that your creative endeavor will produce some kind of finished product. Last, that the end product of your creative endeavor will provide a service to someone else. A song that others may hear. An aesthetically pleasing building that others will inhabit. A scarf that will warm someone or brighten the day of those who see it.

If these three things are operative, as they often are with knitting, Peg said that you will have tapped into the mysterious recipe for human happiness.

 Try This

Give in to the luxury of meditation by doing a straightforward afghan that doesn't take too much attention. Use large needles (size 10 are good) and a bulky weight yarn. Cast on until proper width is attained, being sure the number of stitches you're using can be divided by 4. Now work the Trinity Stitch (instructions are given at the beginning of Chapter 5). Keep at it until your lap and legs and feet are covered. When the size looks right, cast off.

chapter four

Ripening the Intellect

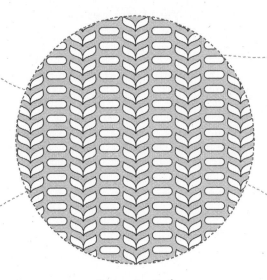

Simple Rib

Ribbing is often used for sweater waistbands, cuffs, and necks. The fabric has a great deal of elasticity and holds snugly to its shape. For easiest results, use this rib over an even number of stitches (multiple of 2).

Row 1: knit 1, purl 1—repeat this sequence all the way across

Row 2: knit 1, purl 1, so that you are knitting the purl stitches and purling the knit stitches of the previous row.

The Waldorf School

It's a windy, warm May morning and I'm driving the streets of Northridge, California, site of the massive 1994 earthquake, looking for Highland Hall School. I pass strip malls by the dozen, gas stations, and stucco houses, mile after mile of flat sameness. I'm awash in four lanes of Balboa Boulevard traffic, a horn-shrieking jumble of morning commuters late to work, looking for a street I can't find. This is the Valley, the San Fernando Valley in all its prototypical suburban sprawl Valley-ness, and I can't help wondering if I'll actually find the idyll I'm looking for.

The street name I'm expecting suddenly appears, and I screech to the right to make the turn.

Highland Hall, a preschool through twelfth grade Waldorf School, is tucked half a block away from the cacophonous street I've just left and is a world unto itself. I pull my car into the gravel-lined parking lot and notice the mothers bringing their children to school. They don't fit the stereotype for Valley mothers—women dressed serviceably in T-shirts, denim shorts, and running shoes, soccer-Mom-types driving Suburban-filled carpools, looking harried and tired. These women are dressed in flowing dresses and wide-legged linen pants, most with floppy straw hats. Many carry wicker baskets of school supplies on one arm, maybe a toddler nestled on the opposite hip. They don't rush the little ones along, but saunter with them to class.

I get out of my car and look around. It's like no citified school I've ever seen. There are rambling hilly areas covered in dewy grass. Trees—not block walls or chainlink fences—provide a natural boundary for the school property. Next to the parking lot is a large vegetable and flower garden. I take my time, wandering around, wondering what it would be like to attend school here. There is an outdoor stage in one area, like a little amphitheater in the wild. I pass a full-sized fort made of logs and more than a few treehouses. This is where the children play. It's like a fairy tale, a magical world just this side of the "real" world. Smaller children, probably preschoolers, are gamboling in the dirt, digging with sticks, racing up a hillside. There are meandering paths that connect the classrooms, dotted now with signs for May Fair 2001; a huge Maypole is the center of the common grass area. I walk to the paved area above the parking lot and find basketball and volleyball courts. A few older kids, high-schoolers, are playing basketball. One boy wears a mammoth curly black wig that bobs when he shoots the ball. From this vantage point, I can see the neighborhood that backs up to the property—all new tract-style homes built on a mansion-sized scale, some crafted to look like a Hollywood imitation of a French chateau. The school seems anachronous in this neighborhood, but blessedly so. I walk back through the parking lot, looking for the school office, and pass a van with an auspicious license plate frame. "I'd rather be knitting," it proclaims, and I know I've come to the right place.

Years ago, when I'd be waxing poetic on the joys of knitting, my sister, who was then working on a master's degree in educational psychology, told me about the Waldorf Schools—an educational movement pioneered by the Austrian scientist and thinker Rudolf Steiner (1861–1925), also known as Steiner Schools—and their philosophy on knitting. It seems that knitting and other handcrafts, including cross-stitch, crochet, and wood-working—are integral to the educational process, with students studying at least one form of handcraft per year, emerging from their educational pursuits with a vast knowledge of how things work and a degree of competence as creators of handcrafted objects.

According to Steiner's philosophy, humans are threefold beings comprised of spirit, soul, and body whose capacities unfold in three developmental stages on the way to adulthood: early childhood, middle childhood, and adolescence. Waldorf philosophy believes that we are more than just a brain, but beings with hearts and limbs, that we are comprised of will and feelings as well as intellect. Hence, art and practical skills are part of the core curriculum, providing an education not only of the heart and hand, but of the brain as well.

Typically, Waldorf schools follow a curriculum based on an ascending spiral—the children engage the same subjects throughout their education on ever-deepening levels. Currently, there are more than 600 Waldorf Schools in thirty-two countries and there are more than 150 schools and initiatives affiliated with the Association of Waldorf Schools of North America, as well as one public Waldorf program in Milwaukee, Wisconsin, and handfuls of charter schools in the United States that use the Waldorf methods.

I've come to this particular Waldorf School on this day to meet Elizabeth Seward. When first researching this book, I attended a class on "Spinning Wool as Spiritual Craft." I took the instructor's name and number, hoping to reconnect with her in the future. Meanwhile, I investigated the handwork teacher at Highland Hall. I'd also asked the monks at St. Andrew's Abbey—a Benedictine monastery in the high desert of California, where I like to go for a spiritual respite—if they knew of any knitters who used the craft to enhance their spirituality. They put me in touch with an oblate of the abbey who was very involved in knitting.

The spinning instructor, the Waldorf handwork teacher, and the abbey oblate—all turned out to be the same person: Elizabeth Seward.

I find Elizabeth in a main office, just ending some kind of conference. I recognize her from the spinning class the moment I hear her speak. She has a quiet, flowing British accent that is undergirded with a certain strength. The softness in her tone makes you feel that everything is right with the world and that you've finally come to the place you've been seeking, while the muscular timbre of her speech—she's direct, almost to the point of sharpness—gives a sense of the iron underlying that gentleness.

Elizabeth is a large woman, the paradigmatic earth mother with rounded curves and a cozy-looking fullness; she's someone you'd want to hug. She favors flowing skirts and dresses of linen and other natural fibers and casual shirts decorated with lace collars. She has a pinkish face surrounded by chin-length nearly white-blonde hair, which looks as soft and wavy as the wool she spins; an easy laugh sings regularly from within her.

To get our knitting conversation rolling, she tells a joke. "There's this van full of children weaving down the highway." A patrol officer sees the van pass by and is concerned. He pulls alongside the vehicle, trying to get the driver to stop. The driver, though, is oblivious. The officer shouts, but the driver doesn't hear. Finally, using the bullhorn on his patrol car, he commands, "Pull over. Pull over!" The driver responds by holding up the knitting she's been working on while driving. "Not a pullover," the driver answers. "Socks."

We laugh a moment before moving into the territory we're here to discuss: why the Waldorf School teaches knitting as part of its curriculum and what this practice accomplishes. I've researched the school's knitting tradition via several publications about Waldorf schooling and learned the basics, including the fact that first graders learn to knit prior to learning to write or to manipulate numbers as a way to develop fine motor skills and numerical understandings necessary for writing and math. Recent neurological research has confirmed that mobility and dexterity in the fine motor muscles, especially those of the hand, may stimulate cellular development in the brain, and, the reasoning goes, strengthen one's ability to think and make intellectual connections. Rudolf Steiner, the founder of the Waldorf School traditions, in fact, has said that "thinking is cosmic knitting."

There are two particular stages at which knitting is prescribed in the Waldorf tradition. The first graders do simple two-needle flat knitting to prepare for writing and math. Holding and manipulating the wooden needles is a good precursor to holding and manipulating a pencil; while the act of counting, decreasing, and adding stitches lays the foundation for later math work.

Later, in fifth grade, the children will reapproach knitting but from a circular perspective, working on four needles to create something to be worn that takes the shape of some part of the body—socks are a common choice. These activities tie together the children's learning about mathematical progressions.

When a child knits, the needles are held in both hands and each hand is assigned a particular activity, according to "Knitting and Intellectual Development," an essay by Eugene Schwartz in *Waldorf Education: A Family Guide*. This action immediately establishes laterality, as well as the eye's control over the hand. The right needle needs to enter a fairly tight loop of yarn on the left-hand needle, weave through the loop, and pull it away onto the other needle. "Only a steady hand can accomplish such a feat, so the power of concentration is aroused," Schwartz writes. The attentiveness required for knitting engenders a degree of concentration that will go far in supporting the children's problem-solving abilities in later years. Additionally, counting the number of stitches and rows needed reinforces and makes tangible math concepts, while using different colors and changing row lengths encourages attentiveness to numbers as well as flexibility in thinking. The child also receives a sense of self-esteem from making something practical and beautiful as the result of learning a new skill.

As Elizabeth explains it to me, first graders knit and work with one thread, learning all the different things that can be done with that one thread. The fifth graders, knitting in the round, learn a different perspective on what they've already learned. They learn that things can be viewed in a more complex light. It's a way of reapprehending something and going deeper into an understanding of it, she explains. "This learning in a deeper manner coincides with the ages of eleven and twelve, which traditionally have been seen as rite-of-passage ages." Many religious and Native American traditions recognize the need for children at this age to begin to take on new and more grown-up roles in life, she explains. In between those two grades, the children will crochet, which requires not manipulating the next stitch that presents itself, but making a choice at every step—where will I make the next stitch? Each of these activities, as well as the cross-stitch and woodworking the children do, are meant to build on each other, creating a sense of confidence in the child, not only in his or her handcraft work, but in making decisions, visualizing problems in a new way, and looking at things from a different point of view.

Elizabeth and I talk about the spiritual aspects of knitting—not necessarily a part of the school's philosophy but a subject we have in common, and one that can't be easily teased apart from the other aspects of the craft—as we wind through the paths to the handcraft room where all the knitting and other supplies are kept. Elizabeth is an oblate at St. Andrew's Abbey, which, she explains to me, "is like being a cousin to the priory, part of the extended family." Many of the oblates pray the liturgy of The Hours, which parallels monastic life, and this practice keeps the lay cousins in constant awareness of the monks at the abbey. Oblates enter the process and study the Rule of St. Benedict, learning what it means to be an oblate and practicing that in one's own life. The oblates then take a solemn profession in which they state their promise to be obedient to the Rule to the degree their station in life allows.

"The Rule of St. Benedict calls for manual labor," she explains when I ask about how knitting impacts her spiritual life. One should earn one's living by manual labor, and there should be a balance between quiet study and participating in the community and church. Some oblates make books, she explains, and others do other things. She knits. "It's like praying with beads, stitch by stitch." This activity connects her to the earth and serves as a form of manual labor. "It's a way of using my head, my heart, and my hands," Elizabeth says. By knitting, we "attach ourselves to the divine, to each other, and to the earth, all of which are essential."

Our conversation weaves back and forth between intellectual development and spiritual expansion, focusing on her view of knitting as a form of empowerment. "It's about being able to clothe oneself," she says and then relates that concept to the monastic tradition of entering a religious life when the person takes on a "habit" and is "clothed" as part of the ritual. That person is then shown to the community as a new person. "It says 'here I am.' The clothes, then, become a physical vessel for the interior state." When children are able to clothe themselves, they sense their own power and their ability to reflect their interior selves in their outward appearances. There is great personal authority in those acts.

These days, with her job training other Waldorf handwork teachers and working with the individual classes, Elizabeth's own knitting time is often less for calm meditation than for figuring out how best to teach the children. "I'm thinking of how to pass on what I know to the children. How is Susan going to be able to do this? Will Mark need a different set of instructions to follow what I'm doing? How will they each learn what I'm trying to teach them in the best way?"

In teaching the children to knit—or anything else for that matter—Elizabeth clothes the lesson in story. Each class time has a story element that weaves together the children's tasks. For example, when teaching children to cast on, she tells a story of a bird on a fence and then gets the children to "catch the yarn like a bird on the fence." Casting off is frogs jumping over each other; the children learn to replicate the frogs' actions with their needles. To teach the basic knit stitches, she has a story about a lamb who was lost. "The shepherd loves the sheep and uses his crook to bring the stranded sheep back to the fold. I tell them how every sheep is important." Elizabeth uses a rhyme to help the children remember the motions of the knit stitch, visualizing a sheep stuck on the other side of a fence and the shepherd's crook gently guiding the sheep back. "Under the fence/catch the sheep/pull him through/away he leaps."

There are many reasons for the decision to teach young children knitting. Elizabeth tells me that the speech center in the brain is right next to the finger center. Speech is very closely associated with knitting. "Come to my first-grade class sometime and you'll see the kids get very talkative when knitting." All this ties together with the fine motor skills. There's another element, beyond intellectual development and motor skills.

"We have a human drive to make things," she explains. "It's something basic to our nature." Plus, handwork is attractive to watch; people stop to look.

I'm thinking of all the things we've discussed when she opens the door to the handcraft room and shows me the wall of yarn that lives just the other side of massive cupboard doors: Shade after beautiful shade of lightly spun pure wool is stacked, organized by color, from the floor to the ceiling. It's a yarn sensualists' treasure trove. I'm awed and inspired. I reach out to touch one color and can't move away from the wall of yarn until I've touched them all. Elizabeth just watches me, knowingly. "We never use synthetics," she explains as I fill my senses with color, touch and texture, drinking in the cache of stunning yarn. Elizabeth holds out a large, round, basketlike wicker platter that's covered in a rainbow of organized cross-stitch thread. It's a feast for the eyes, the way the colors step from one to the next, separated, and yet the ends twining together for a prismatic effect. I stop fondling the yarn to look at the colors.

"We *need* sensual things," she explains as I ogle the deep shades of orange and purple and plum and persimmon. "Natural fibers meet our need for sensual stimulation." Elizabeth says that synthetic fibers fool our senses. We think we're knitting with something real and wholesome, but it might just be the same plastic as a two-liter soda bottle. Synthetics fool us, and we can no longer trust ourselves to recognize what's real and what isn't.

"It's about discernment," she explains. "We teach children to discriminate between wool and synthetics, between wool and other natural fibers. If they're able to discern what's real and what's not in this material realm, they'll be better able to discern what's real—life-giving and life-sustaining—in their life choices. When they make choices about people, about morality. They can sense artificiality in the world better for having learned to discern between things; they're not as easily fooled. They don't sit there wondering, is this a sweater or a soda bottle?" Plus, she points out, it's important for kids to connect with the physical world around them, and what better way than by using natural fibers?

"When kids learn to be creative with their hands, to fill their world with sensual delights like this yarn and these colors, they don't have to rush into being creative—literally—with their bodies prematurely. We need sensuality, and we *can* get it from attentiveness to the world."

The flip side goes unsaid: that if we don't get sensuality from our world, we'll look for it in ways that may not always be healthy or fulfilling.

"It's amazing what kids can learn to do with two sticks and a ball of yarn," Elizabeth says. "They coordinate their left and right hands, getting them both going simultaneously. They develop a focal point, which is crucial for reading. They learn the 'winding around' gesture, which is circular, encompassing, pulling the world into the self, showing one's relationship to the world."

Elizabeth leads me on a tour of the campus. As we walk, I hear a bell chiming and children coming out of classrooms. The bell makes a beautiful, resonating sound, similar to the bell tolling at the abbey, and not at all the jarring electronic ring that I'm accustomed to at schools I've seen. I watch as recess begins. The kids drink from what at first looks like a typical drinking fountain, until I notice the reverse osmosis filtration system leading to the water outlet—even the water here is purified. I point out the treehouses I noted earlier this morning. "They were built in the early 1960s, when the campus was established," Elizabeth explains. "It helps kids to find a home on earth, keeps them physically rooted," she says of the play equipment. The school day, she tells me, is divided into two main sections to better the opportunities for learning. The morning is dedicated to thinking activities, while the afternoon is for more practical work.

We approach the garden by the parking lot I'd noticed earlier, and Elizabeth tells me it's a biodynamic garden, which she says might be considered "beyond organic." It honors the rhythms of the seasons, always plowing the goodness back into the soil. "We plant what the soil needs so that the garden's self-sustaining. We rotate the crops to enrich the soil." Right now, it's mostly flowers. Weeds pop up here and there; some of them are big but don't seem to be bothering anyone. There are a few herbs and vegetables as well. There is a mosaic being constructed as a path around the garden, a work of art and love by one of the parents, using colorful bits and broken pieces of pottery set in cement.

Elizabeth walks me back to the handcraft room, where I plan to spend the afternoon reading the books she's accumulated and getting accustomed to the school. "Teaching children to knit is the best gift I could have," she tells me in a moment of candor. There was this one little girl who was always so active and busy, she says, who finally got the hang of knitting and was just enthralled. "'Mrs. Seward,' the girl said to me one day, 'this is really exciting, isn't it?', and her face was alive with the joy of creating. There aren't many other gifts that could top that one."

I ask if I can come back on a day when she's knitting with the first graders and fifth graders. We schedule a date and Elizabeth leaves me back in the handwork room with the wall of yarn to myself; she's got a meeting to attend and I've plenty of reading to do.

I spend the afternoon reading books of sheep riddles with titles like "Here's to Ewe" and storybooks that have knitting or sheep as a focal point. One in particular, *The Long Red Scarf,* tells of a grandfather who wanted a scarf of his own but couldn't get anyone to knit it for him. He finally learns to knit himself in order to have the scarf he needs to keep him warm and ends up knitting for all the members of his family, sitting with his retired buddy, who also knits. The lesson seems to be if you can knit for yourself, you will find a new sense of power and self-containment lurking within you.

As I read, the room fills with the muffled, octave-ascending sounds of "me, me, me, me, me, me, me, me"—a choir warming up, accompanied by a piano. The high school choral group practices next door and the music is heavenly.

The bookmark in the book I'm reading says: "The answer is not what is always most important."

I feel centered and as if all's right with the world while I'm here. It's the same feeling I get when I go on retreat at St. Andrew's Abbey. It's a fairy tale feeling, one that's enriching and invigorating, but which I know won't last. I'll have to leave here soon and face the real world again. I can't help but wonder what it would be like to spend your everyday life in a place like this. Would the magic grow old, seem commonplace? I pack up my things to leave and on my way out hear a strong bass beat pounding out of a classroom, with brass, woodwinds, and a piano keeping time. I climb on the nearby retaining wall to look in. There's a full orchestra gathered, practicing, with a singer belting out a big-band era song, live music filling the area during the kids' afternoon recess time.

This is like no school I've ever experienced. When I'd asked about the tuition rates, Elizabeth had shaken her head. The fairy tale was expensive. The irony, she'd told me, is that the families are asked to have the children abstain from television watching and video-game playing, to better preserve the children's rich imaginations and not reduce their attention spans to thirty-second increments. But because of the school's location and the cost of tuition, most of the kids who attend are the children of television and movie executives. "If I didn't teach here," Elizabeth explained, "my children couldn't have afforded to go to school here."

Before I drive back across the Valley to pick up my kids from their asphalt-lined urban campus where there's hardly a tree to be seen, I stop at a local knitting shop and buy each of my three children a ball of lightly spun wool similar to what they had at the Waldorf School. I choose variegated colors, a different palate for each child. Perhaps I can't give them treehouses and full orchestras during recess time, but some good wool and hands-on time knitting with their mother is within my power.

Knitting with First Graders

It's late in the school year, the tail end of May, when I return to Highland Hall, my knitting in hand, to spend time with the first- and fifth-grade classes. Elizabeth passes me a massive basket filled with balls of yarn; there are two school mothers here to help as well as another handcraft teacher. We're to enter the room, Elizabeth explains to me, stand at the front in a line, and Elizabeth will introduce each of us. We're to say "Good morning, first grade" when introduced.

When we enter the first-grade classroom, the first thing I notice is the low trestle tables that serve as desks, two students per table, and the beautiful drawings on the board, done in colored chalk. Though I've known colored chalk has existed for years, I'm stunned by how much its use brightens the otherwise typical greenish chalkboard. Why don't other schools make their chalkboards as beautiful? I wonder. Half of the chalkboard is visible to me, decorated so carefully. A curtain that hangs just inches from the chalkboard's surface shields the other half. The teacher can use the curtain to keep distracting information from being introduced at particular times. I wonder if he decorates this second chalkboard anew each day, giving the kids a glimpse later in the day.

The children have just come in from recess and they're hot and sweaty; summer's definitely on its way. As they settle at their desks, many kick off their shoes and wriggle their toes in the soft pinkish carpet. Not only are the floors carpeted, but the walls are tinted in soft tones, sponge-painted; incandescent lamps topped with earth-tone lampshades gently illuminate the room. No jarring fluorescent lights with their interminable buzz. The trestle table desks are made of a light golden wood, and each child has a wooden chair, just the right height.

"Good morning, first grade," I say to the children when I'm introduced.

"Good morning, Mrs. Murphy," they respond, looking at me with frank curiosity.

After introductions, the knitting begins in little clumps of children. I sit by Stefan, a boy of about seven with India ink eyelashes, blunt freckles, and golden brown hair who wants to show me the blanket the class has made. He holds it out to me with obvious reverence, though the blanket is beginning to fall apart in sections, the stitches having been worked loose by lots of love and wear.

"I did the white square," he announces proudly. The blanket is a melange of light blue, pale green, and white, pieced together and edged by an adult hand in crochet.

"I did a white one and a blue one," another child tells me, a group having gathered near this stranger to the classroom.

"I made three of the squares," a different boy reports.

"Did you see Lawrence's lion?" Stefan asks. "He's almost done with it. He's doing the mane now."

The children are making either lions or lambs, their choice, following a pattern that is nearly the same for either animal. The selection of color and finishing elements are what makes the difference.

"What are you making?" I ask Stefan.

He holds his knitting out to me. "A lion," he says with awe at the fact he could make such a thing. "It's golden."

I sit with Stefan and help him with his knitting when he gets stuck. He's at the part where he must cast on eight additional stitches for the next two rows in order to form the lion's back legs.

"Are you a teacher?" he asks after getting used to my presence.

"No," I tell him. "I'm a writer."

He thinks about this piece of information for a moment and then responds: "I'm talented in climbing."

We knit quietly, and I notice the brightly colored hand-knit flute cases hanging by long chain-stitched cords. The children have knit their own flute cases earlier in the year, and the classroom is now brightened by their presence. There are fresh flowers and thriving plants in the room. I notice Stefan staring at me intently.

"Why do you have a little crack there?" he asks, gently touching my face, pointing to the smile lines beside by mouth, creases that are beginning to grow deeper by the year.

"Because I smile a lot," I tell him, and he seems satisfied with the answer.

As Stefan knits, he mumbles the rhyme to himself: Under the fence, catch the sheep, pull him through, away he leaps.

"How many do I need now?" he asks, thrusting his knitting to me to see if he's reached the eight new stitches he's trying to achieve. I count out loud so he can see his progress.

"Three more," I tell him.

He shakes his head in a kind of feigned world weariness. "It's always three more!"

The children around us are knitting in groups, some telling stories to each other. One group breaks out in spontaneous song. "Oh, what a beautiful morning!" six little voices sing. "Oh what a beautiful day!"

At Stefan's urging, I investigate Lawrence's lion, which is just being finished. Lawrence and a girl who's making a lamb are the first in the class to finish their animals. The girl offers her lamb to me to hold. It has a red ribbon tied around its neck. The animals are stuffed with fluffy lamb's wool and feel soft and warm to the touch.

"Lawrence," one of the helper teachers tells him, "you can pick another animal to make now."

Lawrence thinks for a moment before choosing. He leans over to a male classmate and confides, "I'm starting on a lamb," he says, "so my lion will have something to eat."

I learn later that the red ribbon tied around the girl's lamb is a protective device. Lambs with ribbons can't be eaten by stuffed lions.

It's inspiring to watch these children as they learn to trust their own creativity, knowing that if they take the time, they can accomplish a lion-sized task. They are six and seven years old, and yet they're mastering that rare quality, concentration. They are also building elements of self-esteem that cannot easily be unraveled. Completely at ease with the tools they're using, the children are confident making changes and choices about their creations. These are budding artists, I see, digging into the work of life.

I watch another boy finger crocheting what looks like a very long jump rope. The boys in this group are gathered around one of the helper moms. "Will you show us your tattoo?" they ask her.

"If you finish up first," she responds.

They do as bidden and she shows her ankle, the tattoo resting just above it. "It's a Chinese symbol," she tells them, "for happiness and good health." They stare. "Watch," she says, "I'll polish it up." She puts two fingers in her mouth to wet them and then rubs the area of the tattoo with her fingers. Sure enough, the Chinese symbol begins to almost glow. The kids are mesmerized.

We've been knitting for forty minutes when Mrs. Seward calls for our attention. She announces the lamb and lion that have been completed this day and has the children hold them up for praise. "We're going to wait until five animals are ready," she tells them, "before we take them home. Maybe by the next class, we'll be there. Just like we all waited to start kindergarten at the same time, even though some children were older or felt ready sooner. We waited until everyone was ready." The children nod in assent. Mrs. Seward tells a story to end class, using the same Jane and Jeremy characters she invented to teach the children the movements of knitting—they're the characters that use their crooks to catch the lost sheep. The story has a

cliff-hanger ending: The kids in the tale want to take their knitting on a camping trip and their mother said "no."

"Why is that? I wonder," Mrs. Seward asks. "We'll find out
next class." As the other helpers and I return to our places at the
front of the classroom, our baskets of supplies in our arms, the
kids talk among themselves.

"That was short," one child says of the story.

"When's next time?" another asks to no one in particular.

"Goodbye, first grade," we each take a turn saying.

"Goodbye, Mrs. Seward."

"Goodbye, Mrs. Murphy."

Knitting with Fifth Graders

The fifth-grade classroom resembles the first-grade in that
there's no fluorescent lights, but only incandescent bulbs
behind lovely, natural-toned shades. There is a pile of musical
instruments lumped in a corner of the room, flute and violin
cases, a clarinet or two. Again, the chalkboard is covered with
a colored chalk drawing that is nothing short of glorious. There
are fresh flowers and living plants. The children have personal
water bottles by their seats. The room, though, is a mess. The
helper teacher and Mrs. Seward corral the kids into tidying up.
"They're a bit hyper today," she tells me. These children have
just performed the *Odyssey*—they did a performance last night
and another this morning—and the adrenaline rush is quite
evident.

"We even had a horse," one child tells me about last night's production. "A live horse!"

Trying to imagine a live horse in a school auditorium, I'm doubtful. I look to Elizabeth.

"Yes," she nods, "a horse."

It seems they did the production in the amphitheater I'd seen on my first visit, an open-air performance space that can easily allow a horse to participate.

The children gripe about cleaning up, especially a rowdy group of boys who don't want to be doing this, but eventually they all get started and the clean-up's done in a few minutes. A boy in a wheelchair pulls himself out of the wheelchair and drags himself across the floor, in and out of his chair, to do his part in the cleaning up.

Once the housekeeping is accomplished, the kids settle down and pull out their knitting. This is the grade when they learn to knit in the round, taking the earlier experience and broadening their understanding of it. Many in the group are making socks; a few are making tube-shaped dolls and a couple have a hat going. A group of three boys gathers by one of the windows and pulls their chairs up to the window.

"Can we work outside today?" one asks.

"Not today," comes the answer.

The boys stay at that window for the entire session, watching the "games class" (their equivalent of PE) going on just the other side of the pane. The children constructing hats are working with five large double-pointed needles and seem to be making good progress. One girl is creating the most vibrantly colored sock I've ever seen: Every shade of blue and purple is represented. "I'm working on the second sock," she tells me.

"Does the first one fit?" I ask because I'm always amazed when people make socks that fit.

"It's too tight at the top," she confesses but continues working, as if the tightness will be easily overcome. I pull out my own knitting. With everyone working on something different, my own project—a textured cotton purse for my daughter—won't be a distraction as it might have been with the first-graders. It's comfortable to sit with these children and knit. We start talking about books, my favorite subject, and I'm engrossed in their descriptions of their favorite books and memorable characters. The boys who'd been rambunctious at the start of class, complaining the most loudly about having to clean up the room, are now sitting quietly, captivated by their knitting and the games class they're silently watching. I'm amazed at their ability to center themselves so quickly; they've become models of concentration. These are ten-year-old boys.

One girl is making a tube-shaped doll that's now stuffed with wool and has arms sewn in. She's adding hair, one long, brown strand at a time, deciding how low or high to make the doll's forehead. The girl making the blue and purple sock realizes, after turning the heel, that the foot's too big. She tries it on to assess the problem. Too wide, she decides. The helper teacher comes over to witness the predicament. I'm thinking of all the different things that the helper might tell the girl on how to fix it, working out in my mind what I'd do if the sock were mine. The helper, though, doesn't tell her what to do or give advice.

"What do you think?" she asks the girl. "What could you do to make it work?"

The girl thinks for a moment and announces a set of decreases she could perform to counteract the mistake.

"That might work," the helper says and leaves her to her work.

What an amazing thing: to trust this young girl to figure out the solution to her problem. I'm amazed and pleased, thinking of all the ways I could use this experience in my own life. All the times I try to tell my children or loved ones how to fix their mistakes instead of trusting them to have the brains to figure it out themselves with just a friendly eye to watch over them. Hmmm.

Mrs. Seward announces that time is running out. I can't believe how the time has gone, and neither can the children.

"I want to stay in at recess and knit," says the girl with the blue and purple, nearly completed sock. "I want to finish my sock!"

"Goodbye, fifth grade." We stand at the front of the class.

"Goodbye, Mrs. Seward. Goodbye, Mrs. Murphy."

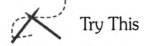 Try This

Make a Waldorf-type animal toy for a child you know or to be donated to a local hospital or police department for a child in need. The pattern below, an approximation of what's used in the Waldorf School I visited, can be adjusted to be a dog, cat, lion, lamb—just about any four-legged creature.

Cast on 36 stitches on size 7 needles with a worsted weight yarn. Knit for 10 rows. Bind off 8 stitches at the beginning of the next 2 rows to form the animal's back legs. Knit for 8 rows on the remaining 20 stitches to make the animal's torso. Over the next 2 rows, cast on 8 new stitches at the beginning of each row. (Do this as if you're casting on at the beginning of a work, adding the new stitches before knitting across the existing stitches.) Knit for 10 rows over these 36 stitches to form the animal's forelegs. At the beginning of the next 2 rows, bind off 12 stitches to form the animal's neck. Knit 24 rows over the remaining 12 stitches for the head, then bind off.

To assemble the animal, sew each leg seam (working on the wrong side), then the torso. Turn it right-side out and stuff the legs before sewing the back end seam. Add a tail at this time if you like. Next, fold the head together and sew across the bound-off stitches, then shape the head by tucking its chin in and sewing in place. Shape the animal with your hand. Add a mane or eyes or ears with extra yarn and a sewing needle.

chapter five

Contented Soul

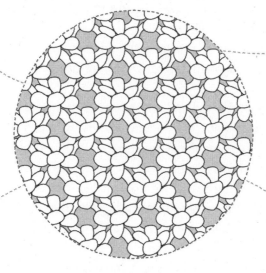

Trinity Stitch

Great texture, perfect for afghans. Must be worked over a number of stitches that can be multiplied by 4.

Row 1: knit 1, purl 1, knit 1 into first stitch, then purl 3
   together—repeat this sequence all the way across.
Row 2 and all even-numbered rows: purl across.
Row 3: purl 3 together, then knit 1, purl 1, knit 1 into next
   stitch—repeat this sequence all the way across.

One of my favorite stories that for me illustrates the connection between knitting and prayer tells of a spiritual seeker interviewing a highly enlightened Buddhist monk, trying to understand the difference between a common life and a life that is infused with spirituality.

"Tell me, great master," the seeker asked. "Before you became so enlightened, what were your days like, how did you live?"

"I chopped wood and hauled water," the great sage replied.

"And now that you're in tune with the harmony of the world, now that you've found nirvana, how do you spend your days?"

"I chop wood and haul water," the master replied.

It isn't so much what we do with our lives as *how* we do it. The attention we pay to the small, often mundane tasks of life can make the difference between a life of drudgery and a life of joyful service. The many, many chores that make up our days are the same as the sage's chopping wood and hauling water. It is our choice whether they are simply chores or a form of spiritual practice, of mindfulness.

The idea that knitting can be a spiritual practice surprises some people, but it needn't. When you think of it, anything done mindfully and with a certain attitude can be a spiritual practice. One of the key indicators of a rich spiritual life is this quality of mindfulness in all activities—paying close attention to what you are doing, and in the act of immersing yourself in the mindfulness, turning off the nonstop chattering in your head.

Cloistered monks go about their daily activities, whether farming, making ceramics, or chopping vegetables for soup with a degree of mindfulness that imbues their actions with an air of the sacred. According to the Rule of St. Benedict, by which Christian monks of the Benedictine and Cistercian order are guided, there must be a balance between prayer and manual labor in one's day, and the manual labor part of the equation is done whenever possible with a prayerful attitude. In the instructions to the Monastery's Cellarer, for instance, the Rule says that the Cellarer "is to look upon the vessels and goods of the monastery as though they were the sacred vessels of the altar." Likewise, all action, all materials, can be seen as tools for one's spiritual practice. It's simply a matter of perspective.

The idea of knitting as prayer developed in my life as a result of the Catholic tradition of praying the rosary but is certainly not limited to that practice nor to that particular faith. Many wisdom traditions follow some sort of bead-prayer or repetition ritual.

I live in a community heavily populated by Armenian immigrants, in a city on the outskirts of downtown Los Angeles with the largest Armenian population outside of Armenia itself. On the streets, the older Armenian immigrants are always dressed with a degree of formality—the women in dresses or skirts, the men in suit coats and hats—and they regularly walk with their hands behind their backs, a set of prayer beads linking the hands, shrouded in a quiet surrender. The beads move, one by one, through their fingers as they walk the grandchildren to school, amble over to the produce vendor for the day's vegetables, or make their way to the park for a communal game of backgammon. This prayer time is not set apart from the rhythms of the day but is an integral part of their lives.

In Buddhism, the simple act of walking is often used as a form of mindfulness practice and is a wonderful way to experience in your body what I'm talking about. Take a moment now and try it: Stand in your bare feet, the better to feel the earth on which we live. Feel your weight and how it's balanced over your two feet. Where does your weight settle: on the balls of your feet, your toes, your heels? Where do you feel most balanced?

Now think about what happens when you walk. In preparing to take a step, for instance, you'll need to shift your weight onto one of your feet. In order to do this, you must choose which foot is to support your weight and then move your hip to align with that foot, relieving the other foot of its burden. At this point, you're still in balance, but it's a more precarious balance than when you were standing solidly on two feet. You will need to proceed through an interval of imbalance now in order to move forward. To take a step requires instability, the risk of falling. You perch between the extremes of equilibrium and disequilibrium and sway your weight forward onto the new foot and finally arrive with a forward momentum that now causes your weight to be balanced on the forward foot. Continue this process, walking across the room, through your back garden, on a woodland trail, amid noisy city streets—see how engaged in this simple day-to-day activity you can become.

Then try the same attention with your knitting.

But is mindfulness necessarily the same thing as prayer? The answer to that question may depend on which religion or wisdom tradition you follow, but I see the two as interrelated. The biblical injunction comes to mind: "Be still and know that I am God." There's something inherent in stillness and quietness and attentiveness that draws one's thoughts to a higher plane.

A Tool for Prayer

Mary C. Gildersleeve is a design artist who owns "By Hand, With Heart," a knitwear design company in Raleigh, North Carolina. This thirty-nine-year-old mother finds her knitting an ideal tool for prayer. "I often find myself praying while I'm knitting," she said. "I think what happens is that I slow down when I knit and allow all around me to 'disappear' until it's me and God chatting back and forth. There are times when I knit in a crowd or while watching a video, but I'm finding it is more peaceful and fun to knit when the babies are napping and the older kids and husband are out. It's a chance to think about my day, my past, my future, and how I'm leading—or not leading—the life I should be. I find that God gets a chance to talk back when I'm plying the 'two sticks and a string.'"

Mary also sees the activity of knitting as reflective of her Creator's spirit within her. "The ability to create something from nothing is a gift from God," she said, pointing out that this present should never be squandered or wasted. When she knits, not only does she find prayer occurring as if of its own accord, but she also finds herself paying more attention to the wonders of the world around her. "By allowing myself to slow down and sit and knit, or draw, or practice a technique, I'm using a gift from God." This state of mind allows her to look at the world God created, to smell the roses, and to try to emulate some of that beauty and goodness in her own handwork.

Many faiths see, in the human desire to create, a reflection of the divine creative spark. Some might say that when we create, when we tap into the wellspring of beauty and aesthetic harmony that surrounds us, we are most in tune with God.

Starting Life in a Paper Bag

Rosemary Porter Capitolo is a fifty-seven-year-old knitter from San Jose, California, and a pastoral associate for Santa Teresa Catholic Church. She starts her day with an hour-long walk and then an hour of knitting as her way of prayer. "Because of my ministry, I was searching for ways to enhance my prayer life," she explained. "Meditation was always touted as being somehow a 'higher' form of prayer. I took many classes and listened to a boatload of tapes, but that 'drunken monkey' was always running around in my head." One morning when she was knitting, she suddenly realized that she was in a meditation "zone." "It was the same zone I'd experienced when I took my early morning walks or when I did tai chi." "Bingo," she thought and decided to do her knitting as a form of meditation and prayer. As a high-energy person, Rosemary said that when her hands (or feet) are doing something else, she is able to quiet her mind. This quiet time pays off for her in many ways.

"A good portion of my ministry is spent with the sick and the dying," she explained, as well as with those people who visit and care for the ill. Thanks to her experience using knitting as meditation, she said that she has learned how to sit quietly and really listen to the people's worries and fears. "I am no longer nervous or concerned about the space between questions and answers," she told me. "I am better able to hear the unsaid."

Her comments remind me of the first job I'd taken after college. I was the public relations representative for a large hospital serving urban Los Angeles, one of the few remaining hospitals in the area that offered a Trauma Center. Because of the Trauma Center's ability to treat extensive injuries quickly, thanks to a comprehensive on-call staff of surgical experts, we received the most critical cases, including many drive-by and gang-related shootings, as well as casualties of horrific car accidents. It was my job to report to the media about celebrity patients, high-profile cases, and the victims of newsworthy events. It fell to me to announce the details of a person's death to the news media, who would then report it to the world, often with my name attached.

More than a few times, the ER physicians would tell me that a particular patient wasn't going to make it; that a specific, individual life had been reduced to "a matter of time." I couldn't report *that* prognosis to the media, of course, because sometimes miracles occurred and the person recovered. Most of the time I'd keep a kind of uneasy vigil, waiting for the person to die so that I could make the formal announcement.

There was something very sacred to me about that time. I'd close my office door, stop all incoming calls, and pull out my knitting. As I made each stitch, I'd think about the soul preparing to leave its body in the emergency room across the courtyard from me. Often, there'd be family members in the ER keeping watch; but sometimes I was the only person beyond the ER staff consciously thinking about this person whom I'd never met and never would meet and offering my own awkward attempts at prayer for the soul preparing to make its crossing. That was when I first became aware of the more sacred aspects of my knitting time.

Previously, I'd known my knitting as a way to relax and engender meditative states, but I'd never before seen it metaphysically. The garments I produced during the vigils were always bittersweet for me, as if my thoughts of that departing soul were now interwoven with the actual stitches. Though I invariably made the phone calls to the media to report the person's death, I felt that I was honoring the individual nature of souls I'd never met in this odd little way.

One of the sweaters I made during that time was a heather brown basketweave wool pullover for my older brother Frank. A few years later, when Frank was in Tahiti doing his job supervising the UC Berkeley biology field station house in Moorea, all his belongings—everything he owned in the world except the clothes that he had with him—burned to the ground in the great Oakland fire of 1991. Because he'd been renting and had no insurance, there was no way for him to recoup the loss. He picked up the thread of his life, though, and moved forward. When I later realized the connection between the fire and my efforts at constructing that particular sweater during a time of so many deaths, having lost it in such a way seemed fitting.

Rosemary, the pastoral associate I interviewed, said the effects of knitting—her own as well as other people's—reflect God's work in her life. Once, while she was working at the local soup kitchen, a young indigent woman came in with a newborn infant. The mother carried her child with all the care in the world, showing off the baby and the beautiful handmade blanket in which the child was wrapped. The young woman told Rosemary that the blanket had been a gift to her at the homeless shelter where she was staying. "She kept telling me how beautiful it was," Rosemary said. "I will never forget the look in her eyes. We all need beauty in our lives."

As if to contrast the heartwarming mien of that story, Rosemary recounted another. "We have a layette group at our church, which provides baby items for families in need. I knit baby hats, blankets, and sweaters for the group. I love knitting, knowing that someone will be able to bring her baby home in something beautiful." At the layette diocesan shower this year, Rosemary said, a young woman told about having to bring her first baby home from the hospital in what she received from the hospital and a paper bag. "No one deserves to start life in a paper bag," Rosemary explained.

That Which You Do to the
Least of My People

Indeed, many wisdom traditions preach our individual and communal responsibilities to help each other and most especially those in need. Works of charity are one of the five "pillars of Islam" that followers are expected to observe. In Christian scripture, we find Jesus thanking his followers for visiting him in prison, giving him food when he'd been hungry and drink when thirsty, offering him clothes when he had none. They retorted, "We never did that." Jesus explained: "Whatsoever you do to the least of my people, that you do unto me." In Jewish scripture, there are repeated commandments to help widows and orphans, to care for the poor and hungry, to celebrate with the bride and groom. In fact, it may be this commandment to care for each other that is one of the most unifying elements of virtually all world religions.

I attended Mitzvah Day at Temple Israel of Hollywood last year. (The word *mitzvah* is Hebrew for "good deeds"; Jews are commanded to perform *mitzvoth,* acts of goodness that are often cloaked in anonymity, for those who are in need as part of their covenant with the Almighty.) The annual day is attended by people of all different faiths; it is a day in which we pitch in together to do good, to heal the world by working communally. Some of the Mitzvah Day groups go to old age homes to sing or read to the residents. Others clean and organize second-hand toys to be donated to needy children, while some participate in soup kitchens. There are jobs for anyone who cares to show up—small children, teens, young adults, the elderly—everyone is given a way to help. The littlest ones decorate Cookie Monster cookies, getting more frosting on themselves than on the cookies. Since even the least effort is valued here, I learn that I don't have to do big things to help heal the world, but I need to do *something*.

My group knitted squares to be joined together as baby blankets for impoverished new mothers. The gathering of knitters was reflective of the scope of this craft. There were professional women—one was an attorney, law school professor, and an accomplished author, another, a professional fashion designer. There were grandmother-types, young girls from the Girl Scout troop of the local Catholic school, teens and young adults from college. Some were expert knitters, others rank beginners. We sat in the room and knitted as all around us good works were being facilitated. My children and husband peeked in to say hi between organizing donated clothing and delivering baskets of household items for homeless AIDS patients moving into their own apartments.

The yarn we used had been donated by local knitting shops, and though the finished blankets may not have been the most spectacular-looking knitwear one could find, they were certainly filled with our love and compassion.

Throughout the day, the talk at the table grew lively. We learned how each of us, all hailing from different traditions, learned to knit. We discussed the lessons passed on by aunts, grandmothers, and mothers. When the teens and young adults got tired of the knitting, they put on some rousing Israeli music and began a line dance they'd learned to celebrate their tradition.

"Bernadette Murphy," joked one of the mostly Jewish women left at the end of the day. "Now that's a good Jewish name!"

I confirmed my Irish-Catholic background. "But I've always felt a particular draw to Judaism," I admitted. "I've considered conversion more than a few times."

"Isn't that funny," piped in another woman, one who had been quiet much of the day. "I was raised Jewish, but always felt more comfortable with Catholicism. All my friends growing up were Catholic," Jane said.

I told her the story of how my children and I tried to hold our own Seder a few weeks earlier at Passover and of the many faux pas we made. Most of my friends, I noted, were Jewish.

"I can't help you with Passover," Jane warned. "But if you have any questions about a First Communion, I'm your girl." Jane and I became friends after that, trading e-mails and making dates for dinner. When we get together, we discuss knitting projects and religion. For reasons I can't always explain, the two, for me, seem to go hand-in-hand.

Buddhist Knitter

Nancy Taylor-Roberts is a fifty-two-year-old knitter in Manchester, Massachusetts, who holds a master's degree in divinity. She worked as a pastoral counselor doing family therapy for many years and seven years ago converted from Christianity to Buddhism. Nancy doesn't see knitting as exemplifying a true form of meditation because for her meditation "implies not doing, just being. So even if I'm not doing anything but knitting, I'm still knitting." However, she explained, she can't say definitively that it's *not* a form of meditation, either. To be a true form of Buddhist meditation, in her estimation, the knitting activity would "have to be very sharply focused on the yarn, the needles, and the movements of the hand." Asked if she viewed knitting as a form of prayer, she replied that, being a Buddhist, she doesn't pray much "except when I feel my life is in danger and I revert to my Christian upbringing reflexively."

As far as tapping into a deeper level of consciousness via knitting, though, Nancy believes there is a correlation. When she knits, she often chooses to be quiet, to "enjoy the woods where I am blessed to live, let thoughts travel in and out of my mind, pay attention to some, ignore others, solve half of the world's problems, remember people I love and have lost. As I think of it," she explained, "the thoughts that come while knitting are calming thoughts. I never knit and feel angry at the same time." She laughs for a moment. "Although there's plenty of anger in me, it seems to respect the sharp objects in my hands." Knitting, though, teaches her how to be in the moment. "Leave the moment," she cautioned, and you'll "make a mistake, suffer, rip, repent. Stay in the moment and watch something beautiful emerge."

It's precisely this process that excites Nancy and that, in its own way, seems to me similar to the process of prayer when the object of prayer is to make connection with the divine. Many mystics have written about the dark night of the soul, the experience of prayer when no one seems to be listening and nothing productive seems to be happening, and the need to persevere regardless. In many ways, prayer isn't intended for God to know our thoughts and desires and praise. Rather we regain awareness of the divine aspects of our everyday lives. Nancy's comments reflect this.

"Every project has its challenges," she said. "In each sweater there are times I get really discouraged or bogged down. There's great satisfaction in sticking with it, moving through the difficult times and getting to the end. Then you just have a thing, and things are impermanent and of little value," she said. "That's the Buddhist in me," she added as an aside. "The experience is more interesting."

And how, exactly, does that experience manifest itself in Nancy's life? "I relax when I knit, even if I'm doing something very difficult or fixing a mistake. I'm sure my blood pressure drops—I've documented that at the doctor's. I imagine my heart rate slows. My mind drifts into calming and soothing thoughts as it moves back and forth between the stitches and the everyday barrage of ideas, memories, problem-solving, and the desire to be fed! I eat when I knit and it slows me down and keeps me from eating too much. A yogurt lasts half an hour while knitting."

Nancy said that her piano teacher keeps a close watch over her because the teacher fears she will injure herself knitting and then not be able to play the piano. She's actually much more interested in not injuring herself playing the piano. But then, Nancy added, her piano teacher isn't a knitter.

Parish Priest Spins and Knits and Prays

Betty Berlenbach, a fifty-seven-year-old Episcopal priest, serves as the parish pastor in Perkinsville, Vermont. Betty responded to my questions and interest in her views on knitting with an amazing generosity of spirit and a profound sense of honesty; she even invited my family out for a visit to enjoy the gorgeous hills of Vermont, to get to know her sheep, and to learn to spin. Though I have thus far been unable to take her up on this generous offer, I have benefited deeply from the insights she shared with me about knitting and religion.

I asked how I was to refer to her as a priest who's a female, since the term "father" doesn't seem to fit. Her down-to-earth manner and exacting honesty revealed themselves right away.

"I've never quite understood why people who are oriented to calling male priests father find it so difficult to figure out the logical female equivalent," she fired back. "If a male is like your father, what might a female be like? Your mother? Actually, I think both father and mother are stupid patriarchal-type terms which imply a one-up position for priest, in comparison with parishioner," she stated, "so I prefer my parishioners to call me Betty, as that is my baptismal name, and it is our baptism which we hold in common in church."

Betty's strong opinions seem to spring from a deep well of prayer, compassion, and hard-won wisdom. She seems the kind of person who doesn't suffer fools gladly, but brings to any genuine discussion a degree of openness and integrity often lacking in contemporary life.

For Betty, the craft of knitting has had four different births in her life. Her first knitting experience was when a Girl Scout leader taught her to knit when she was in fifth grade. She had previously crocheted, a skill her grandmother had taught her. No one in her family knitted. Her introduction to knitting involved creating a scarf, all knit, no purl. "And that was that," she said, until college and the second birth.

"My roommate, who knitted while studying with the help of a book holder, guided me through a sweater for my then-boyfriend, now-husband. When finished, it would have fit Mighty Joe Young, but he sweetly wore it a couple of times before it disappeared. I made a couple of sweaters during college—something to do on the cafeteria line—but all this was following patterns and went no further."

The third birth of her knitting life came during the child-bearing years and shortly thereafter, when she made lots of sweater sets and knitted and crocheted for her children and those of her sisters. She got interested in knitting Icelandic sweaters at that time, but still, she was always following patterns.

It wasn't until a few years ago, when she learned to spin wool, that knitting was born anew in her life. Betty lives on forty-two acres of Vermont hill country, including forest and flat pasture, where she rears fourteen Jacob sheep, eight Shetland sheep, and currently twenty-one lambs. After she discovered spinning, Betty read a couple of books that talked of "Knitting in the Old Way," that is, on circular needles from the bottom up, and pretty much began designing her own patterns, which, she said, "is a whole 'nother ball game." Now she knits in a more holistic way, starting with the sheep, harvesting the fleece, washing it—which is a favorite part of the process—picking it, carding it, spinning it, sometimes dying it, and then knitting it. Usually she begins a sweater knowing what size she wants it, what size needles she will be using, and whether she's going top-down, bottom-up, or in pieces. She decides what neck or waist/hip band pattern she will use. "And then, I just let the sweater unfold, so to speak, letting the wool speak to me, and proceeding as the spirit moves me, as the wool wants to be designed. Sounds a little crazy, I know, but I intuit my way through the sweater." Though she said that every once in a while she'll look at a pattern, incorporating bits from here and there, mostly she just knits. "This kind of knitting is very creative," Betty said, "and doesn't limit me to the boundaries of someone else's pattern and is, therefore, much more likely to be a spiritual type of activity for me, a sharing in creation of beauty."

Betty said that her earlier experiences of "knitting as follow-the-leader" involved only her rational mind, copying someone else's creativity, which for her became problematic. Yes, it created a beautiful garment, and yes, concentrating on doing it right often meant she locked out everything else, which gave a sense of relief from problems, but "it was really just a put-it-off-a-bit strategy," she explained.

After she began engaging with the yarn from the sheep forward, though, things changed. "I know, for example, when I'm knitting with Harriett's fleece, I am connecting with good old Harriett, whose full name is Harriett the Bitch and who is pretty cantankerous at times, but nevertheless a sheep I admire. Nina's beautiful, soft light brown fleece reminds me of her beautiful, soft nature, she being the ambassador of friendship on the farm, willing to approach even total strangers and welcome them by requesting attention: a little ear massage, scratch under the chin, perhaps a little lick of salty skin. Rachel and Rebekah's wonderful black-and-white Jacob fleeces are lustrous and long stapled, a generosity of yummy soft fiber to play with and turn into any number of shades and tints and patterns of rovings or batts to spin and knit."

In spinning and knitting up this fleece from her farm, Betty said it is as if she is in partnership with the sheep who share the land with her. "Together, using both of our gifts, we create beauty and offer it up to the world." Each time she knits from yarn spun from a sheep she knows—hers or a friend's—there is a personal and communal element to the knitting. The act of knitting, for Betty, has gone from being a hobby to an art form and a spiritual practice.

Talking about prayer, Betty said that it has been defined by some as "being in the moment." Given that, she knits at lectures, which keeps her focused on the information at hand. (It's not a time for complicated counting patterns, she warned, but rather the back and forth of rote knitting.) She knits as a calming activity, in the midst of chaos, which enables her to create order as well as beauty somewhere in her life, an aspect she finds reassuring. "Knitting reminds me of certain religious truths which seem to show up in most religious traditions. For example: You *can* rip it out and start over, if need be. There is always another chance."

Even ripping out and starting over, for Betty, is spiritual in that it reminds her that she is honoring the sheep and fleece and not wasting its gifts by tossing a project aside if she doesn't like it. Yarn is a renewable resource, one that can be used over and over again, she said.

"At this point in my relationship with the holy, I find myself not coming away to engage the holy, but entering into instead; entering into natural processes, the forest, etc., recognizing the connectedness of all creation, contemplating smaller and smaller portions of creation, and recognizing that all of creation is present in all of creation."

For Betty, knitting is fertile ground for that contemplation. The yarn she uses often still smells like sheep, since she washes it lightly, deliberately to retain some lanolin and "some sense of sheepiness, and the softness of the fleece, instead of harshly attacking it with chemicals, as commercial yarn manufacturers often do."

Knitting seems to be a metaphor for turning chaos into order, she explained, for communion, for creativity. "Instead of just thinking about these concepts with my rational mind or even moving into contemplation which involves my intuitive mind, knitting involves also my senses and my feelings. This means all four Jungian functions are involved, which is the place Jung suggested that revelation takes place. Mostly, though, it is involvement in and connection to the process of creation in a visceral way instead of a theoretical way."

As an ordained priest, knitting impacts Betty's professional life in many ways. On a purely practical level, she said, knitting is an activity she holds in common with many members of her congregation, a common ground that helps to equalize things between them. "I reject the father-knows-best type of theology which suggests that the priest is the one with the knowledge and position and the congregation is the audience, there to watch the performance. Knitting is one way I can relate to many parishioners." On another level, she donates knitted items to church events, just like the parishioners do, again putting herself on the same level with those to whom she ministers, an idea she feels very strongly about.

"On deeper levels," she said, "I am known in the community as someone with sheep who spins and knits, as well as a priest—that is, a regular person—more than as the holy minister in the black outfit. I almost never wear clerical garb."

She has also preached about knitting or used knitting as a metaphor for the communal Christian life in her sermons, talking "about the holiness of handwork for opening the heart chakra, so that we are open to doing heart work, the work of healing ourselves and each other for the life of the world."

In her other professional life—that of teacher, which preceded and often goes hand-in-hand with her priestly vocation—

she is aware of the value of knitting and other activities that use both hands, to activate and connect both sides of the brain, and hence, give students a leg up in learning to read and do math, a theory acted out in Waldorf Schools around the country. "In fact, when my grandson comes for a week at the end of the month, I am hoping to begin to teach him to knit. He has some difficulty with reading, and I think it may help, particularly if I don't mention that it is remedial work. I only hope that his father, my son, will help him to continue with knitting at home and not let his high testosterone levels dictate that knitting is girls' stuff." She taught both her sons to knit and weave and cook and sew as children, which she believes are invaluable skills for all children to learn.

Her professional life seeps over into her knitting, she said, in that she looks for signs of spirit and holiness everywhere and is aware of the many gifts to be found in knitting. "I have, along with a friend, Judith Esmay, led two retreats entitled 'Knitting as Spiritual Practice,' which have been most successful in helping people get in touch with who they are, connecting with self, others, the world, and seeing the holiness in the activity, as well as finding metaphors for religious concepts. Next month I'm leading another knitting retreat with a yoga teacher. That'll be an interesting experience, I'm sure."

What happens internally, I asked, when Betty knits?

A lot depends on *how* she's knitting. "If I'm in a hurry to finish something and am throwing the yarn, I warm up considerably, which is really good on cold evenings, I can tell you. If I'm knitting at a reasonable rate, while listening to music or watching TV, it clears my mind to listen. If I'm knitting because I've finished dinner and my husband is just cutting up his meat, it keeps me from eating out of sheer boredom, so I don't gain weight! However, in all my knitting, there is a sense of accomplishment and curiosity and wonder at how it will all come together, which yields peace of mind, a good self-sense and self-image. I can't say that I experience a lower heart rate, because I've never checked; same with blood pressure. But there is a feeling of well-being, of accomplishment, of satisfaction, of being in the now."

Betty's favorite knitting projects are sweaters, though she does clean up her scraps once a year by making a slew of socks. She likes making ganseys best—with textures and patterns in one color. "I find it annoying to do patterns in various colors, though I have done it, mostly to prove to myself that I can." She said that she's not adventurous in terms of spinning and knitting fibers other than sheep's wool or learning new techniques. "There is great comfort in making, not the same sweater each time, but similar ones," she explained. Her basic repertoire includes one sweater constructed in a bottom-up manner "for times when I have energy and time for attention to detail and counting." Another is made top-down for plain, often variegated or striped sweaters. She also has a number of easy knitters with no patterns for keeping her hands busy at meetings, and perhaps she'll have "one newish, somewhat different project"—all of which she keeps going simultaneously. She loves cables, as well as the process of dying different color yarns, blending them to make heathers, and then knitting from those yarns. "I am not real interested in projects so complex that I can't knit on them while talking with friends or watching TV or listening to music."

Since discovering her own way of designing knitting projects, she's enjoyed her knitting much more and believes she's gleaned additional insight. "People who learn to create their own patterns seem to be more deeply involved in the making of the sweater and relating it to their lives than those who just follow a pattern to the letter." Though Betty *does* look at patterns to get ideas, she said, "picking up on this bit here and that bit here," her finished sweaters never match up to the pattern pictures, and that pleases her. "It is usually interesting anyway, and I like it better than what originally I saw." For Betty, the sweaters that take her the longest to finish "are those in which I am following a pattern exactly and using store-bought yarn. I avoid these things as much as possible."

Like many knitters I interviewed, Betty finds a joy in the process that is distinct from the finished work. "I love the knitting and find it very satisfying to see the sweater take shape. I love finishing the sweater, doing the tying in of ends, washing and blocking of it. Then it goes in my For Sale pile, for the most part, and I am no longer really connected to it. I very seldom keep a sweater I make. It appears to be more meaningful to the people who buy my sweaters to know that I made it and what sheep it came from than to me. I guess that it is the challenge, the unfolding, the midwifing and birthing, so to speak, of the sweater that is important to me. After it is finished, there is nothing left for me to do with the sweater. I *did* keep one sweater I made this year, for the first time, and I enjoy wearing it, but primarily because it is perfect for the use, not because I made it."

In our conversations, Betty mentioned two experiences that seemed particularly noteworthy. The first was when she and three friends did a "sheep to vest" project at a church bazaar. They had the sheep shorn, did the carding and spinning the wool in the grease, and then knitted a vest in four parts, connecting the parts to form one vest, which was raffled off at the end of the day. "There was a sense of camaraderie, of communal creativity, of just plain fun, watching folks watch us turn this fleece into a garment," she said.

The second experience was one that her friend Judith organized and participated in. She explained: "Having read about some similar thing in the Midwest, Judith decided to take some yarn she had and knit a shawl, a prayer shawl, for a woman in her church who was dying of cancer. Judith intentionally prayed for the woman as she knit. She also got everyone in the choir, of which this woman was a member, and some educational groups, ditto, all to knit at least one stitch, which required her showing them all how to do it, men and women, and to pray for her while they did it.

"The woman loved the shawl, took it with her to the hospital, and if I am not mistaken, it was with her, perhaps on her, when she died. That was a very deeply spiritual experience for Judith and those who knitted on the shawl. She has now involved others in the parish in the desire to do more of these for specific people in spiritual need, if not physical need."

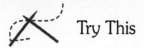 Try This

Make something for someone you're concerned about: a friend who's battling an illness, a parent with whom you're on difficult terms, a stressed coworker, or a high school buddy whose presence you miss. Hold that person close in your thoughts as you knit, concentrating on good things happening in and through that person's life. Make a sacred garment in which to clothe your friend in love and positive, uplifting thoughts. You don't have to tell the person about these thoughts and wishes that are woven into the work. Trust that your intentions will manifest themselves through the act of your knitting.

Basket Stitch

Rows 1 and 7: Knit all the way across.
Rows 2 and 8: Purl all the way across.
Rows 3 and 5: Knit 1, purl 4, knit 1—
   repeat this sequence across all stitches.
Rows 4 and 6: Purl 1, knit 4, purl 1—
   repeat this sequence across all stitches.
Rows 9 and 11: Purl 2, knit 2, purl 2—
   repeat this sequence across all stitches.
Rows 10 and 12: Knit 2, purl 2, knit 2—
   repeat this sequence across all stitches.

chapter six

Creative Spirit

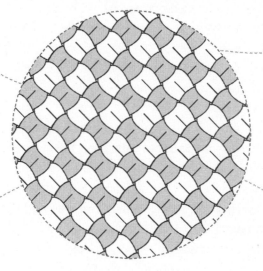

Basket Stitch

This stitch makes a wonderful texture for sweaters, scarves, afghans, etc. It will not roll at the ends the way stockinette stitch will. You work the basket stitch in multiples of six, so be sure the number of stitches you plan to use it on is divisible by six. When working the pattern, the first set of six rows establishes the pattern; the second set of six rows reverses the pattern. Then it repeats.

(see pattern to the left)

Every artist I meet is creative in his or her primary and unique way. Whether we choose to express our art through painting, sculpture, music, writing, filmmaking, fiber art, or the vast welter of artistic outlets available to us, we all bring our idiosyncratic selves to bear on the things we create. Knitting is no different. For some, knitting itself is *the* art, the specific outlet through which one's desire to create is funneled. For others, like myself, knitting is a tool for increasing the depth and creativity of our chosen art form.

Knitting can be the point of connection, the liaison as it were, between our rational minds and our creative selves. Because the knitting mindset creates a place where ideas can germinate and take root in a judgement-free space, inspirational thoughts that pop up during knitting time often bring answers to artistic concerns. It is where inchoate glimmers of ideas can dance before our eyes, tempting us to take seriously things that our rational mind might immediately censor or dismiss.

If nothing else, knitting provides a break from the concentration needed to practice one's art and a sensual, aesthetically pleasing treat after a job well done.

Food as Art

It's a warm, early summer's day in Los Angeles. I drive the few miles that separate my part of the city—demure, cautiously cosmopolitan, and more than a little conventional—to Silver Lake, the district just north of downtown known as a funky artists' enclave. The community surrounds a man-made water reservoir known as Silver Lake, though the lake itself is not available for swimming, fishing, or even walking along its shores. The whole concrete-enclosed basin is surrounded by chain link fences, and locals take to walking the lake's circumference outside of these obtrusive boundaries. I have to be very careful as I drive, lest I run into one of the many who are jogging, walking, or pushing ultra-hip baby strollers along the lake's outer perimeter. The roads wind through Silver Lake, narrow and twisted, inscribed with squiggly patterns made from an oil-based asphalt-patching material—repairs after recent earthquakes, ground settlings, and whatnot. They look like glyphs dotting the streets, portending something intangible.

Silver Lake has been dubbed by many the heartland of hip in Los Angeles. When the Westside areas of Santa Monica and Venice became too pricey and staid for many of their edgy inhabitants, the migration to the east side of the city began in earnest. A big contingent came from West Hollywood, gay couples who were ready to settle down to domestic bliss and escape the nightlife scene. Also, countless artists and musicians who wanted to concentrate on their work without the Westside distractions moved in as well. Silver Lake is home to the alternative rocker Beck, who hit it big a few years ago; the neighboring community to the north, Los Feliz, was made popular as a hipster hangout in the film *Swingers*. In the last ten years, Silver Lake has morphed from an inexpensive neighborhood with crime problems and many unkept houses, to a hipified community of artists, filmmakers, musicians, writers, and other bohemian types.

My stepbrother is one of these bohemians, a director of commercials, and it's he that first told me about Clare Crespo. He knew Clare from the commercial-making world. She'd been the executive producer at Propaganda Films and someone with whom he often worked; she was well connected in the "industry."

"She's in a knitting bee with all kinds of celebrity people, like Sophia Coppola," David had said. According to his report, Clare meets regularly and knits with some of the most highly respected film-industry women he could think of. But it wasn't the fame of her knitting cohorts that had intrigued him in the first place, but what she did with her craft.

"She knits food," he'd explained.

I didn't get it. Did he mean she took pieces of actual food and used needles to make them into something?

"I was on a flight to New York with her, and she pulled out her knitting supplies," he explained. She used just regular yarn—no actual food products. "As we chatted, she knit a whole plate of sushi, chopsticks, a piece of wasabi, and all."

I still had trouble envisioning what he was describing, but after lots of David explanations, I started to get it: Clare creates three-dimensional stuffed representations of various kinds of food. Her hand-crafted plates of eatables have been featured in Los Angeles art galleries, David told me. "She's become an L.A. artist to watch."

I tried to imagine shaping food with yarn and my knitting needles and still couldn't quite make the leap. "How can you knit food?" I asked.

"I don't know," he laughed, as if I expected him to name the pattern or stitch he'd seen her use. "But she did. Solid, pick-'em-up-and-hold-them pieces of sushi."

It turns out that David doesn't know his knit from his purl because Clare actually creates the food using yarn and a knit-like stitch, but she does so with a crochet hook, not knitting needles. Clare and I had traded e-mails about her knitted/crocheted food before today's actual meeting. Initially, I'd been disappointed because I'd wanted these stories to focus exclusively on knitting, and if she used a crochet hook, how did that fit in? She described her work, though, as something that even avid knitters couldn't always peg as knitted or crocheted. She said she'd been taught to crochet by her grandmother but couldn't remember exactly how to do it, so that when she took up making the food in this manner, the stitch didn't turn out the proper way. This resulting stitch seems to be a hybrid between knit and crochet, with the look of garter stitch, but done in such a way that she can adjust for shape more easily than with straight knitting.

I locate Clare's address on a windy, tree-pocked Silver Lake street and park. The house is stacked, like many in the area, with the garage on the ground floor and the living quarters above it, beginning on the second floor. I can see her from the street; she's talking on a cordless phone from her bedroom, her head near the window. She waves hi and tells me to come on up.

Mounting the stairs, the wrought-iron banister in hand, the first thing I notice is a flock of crows roosting near her front door. Seriously: There are five very lifelike crows perched on the top of the iron railing right next to her front door. I have to walk past them to get in. Upon closer investigation, I see they're counterfeit crows. Their actual feathers and beady bright eyes, though, are surreally convincing.

"Leftovers from Halloween," Clare explains when she opens the door and sees my surprise. She put them up for Halloween last year, she explains, and never got around to taking them down. Now, she's grown rather fond of them. For Christmas, she'd put red bows around their necks. Currently, a few sport green Mardi Gras–type beads. "This is for St. Patrick's Day," she says, though currently it's June. The crows are a bit dusty but still amazing.

"Not too long ago, I heard this incredible racket out here and came to see what was going on." She gestures to the large tree that intrudes a bit on her front doorstep. "There were all these crows hanging out there." She'd never seen a single crow in that particular tree before. "They thought I was having a crow party!" Laughter percolates from within her. "They were mad that I didn't invite them!"

Clare is thirty-three years old but looks to be in her twenties. She has long, medium-blonde hair, pulled back now in a simple ponytail. She's small, short of stature and light of build, dressed today in a funky tight blue T-shirt and jeans, her feet in thongs. She wears no makeup and has a very open, expressive face. Over the course of the morning, the thing that'll register the most with me is how frequently and freely she laughs.

Her dog Zep bounds out to meet me. Big and friendly, he is both gentle and unabashed; he licks my hands when I reach down to pet him, and when I follow Clare into the living room, he licks my ankles. Clare shoos him away.

The living room is contemporary with stacks of books and CDs lining the walls. The walls themselves are painted in bright colors: one is green, another red, another orange. The furniture is art-deco, including butterfly chairs, but the result is not a studied décor done for effect. Clearly, it's a relaxed, working home.

Before we get to the knitted/crocheted food-as-art I've come to see, Clare shows me her current project. She's been contracted to create a cookbook of fun, weird food that will do double-duty as a coffee-table art book. The photographic proofs are all around the room, as are some of the food models. She's done a fish aquarium filled with Jell-O and edible fish. For the photo shoot, she explains, they didn't use the gummy fish she'd listed in the recipe, but fake fish and a plastic aquarium plant. The effect is wonderful. There's a photo of two cakes, one made to look like a pair of pants, the other a brightly striped shirt, laid out on a clothes dryer. Her "monster mashed potatoes" peer out, menacingly, from under her bed in another photo.

"Are the mashed potatoes really on the carpet?" I ask, because they look like they are.

"It's kind of disgusting, isn't it?" Actually, the potatoes were placed on a sheet of cardboard for the photo shoot, she explains, but says she's been feeling weird whenever she gets out of bed lately, convinced that the potatoes might actually be lurking there somehow. The photos were all taken in her home.

Clare's art/cookbook, *The Secret Life of Food,* is due out in spring 2002 from Hyperion. It's another one of her projects that combine her two favorite things: food and art. (You can see her weird food and get odd recipes at her Web site: *www.yummyfun.com.*)

We sit down to talk about knitted food. Clare pulls examples from a box: plate after plate of representational food she's created with yarn, a crochet hook, bathroom-type cotton balls for stuffing, and loads of imagination. A T-bone steak sits on a yarn, constructed plate, cozying up to a fat baked potato that's topped with a perfect square of butter. Next, a fruit platter, featuring a chunky, three-dimensional watermelon wedge standing on its rind, pointing to the ceiling. Beside the watermelon she places a fat purple plum and a half-peeled banana who's yarn-constructed peel just asks for a tug. I hold the pieces and squeeze them in my hand. They're playful, like a preschooler's plastic food and make-believe kitchen set. They make me want to stage a fantasy picnic.

"This is my snack cake plate," she says of the next one.

I'm puzzled by the first item, a fat disk of silver glittered yarn topped with brown and a white squiggle.

"A Hostess cupcake," she explains. There's a Twinkie, a Ding Dong, and the requisite glass of milk.

Where do these delightfully odd ideas come from?

It's the colors that get her going, she explains. "Look at this." She shows me a medium dark pink yarn. "I saw this and all I could think of was smoked salmon." Clare pulls out a yarn plate and then positions a pair of two-toned bagels, dark on the top and lighter on the bottom, on it. She adds pieces of lox, crafted from the exact pinkish yarn she's put in my hands, onto the bagel platter. Next, there are tomato slices, cut up bits of red onion, and a lemon wedge. "I'd go into yarn shops looking for interesting colors and the ladies there would ask, 'Honey, what are you working on?' and I'd lie to them. How could I explain this?" She gestures to the plates of fabricated food filling the coffee table. "I didn't want the ladies to think I was making fun of them."

To be certain, Clare *was* making fun, but it was the art world as a whole she was lampooning, not ladies who knit. She explains.

Clare did her graduate studies at Cal Arts, an exclusive, pricey, Southern California university that specializes in fine and commercial arts. She found the art world to be "snotty, too exclusive, too uppity. It intimidated me." She wanted art and the experience of viewing art to be much more universal than what she'd encountered. "I think everything in life can be art, most especially food." She set out, not to create something that only high-brow art experts would "get," but to "make art that my grandmother and my young cousin could understand." Clare wanted to create things that would appeal to people who weren't "art people."

Lest this description imply that Clare set out to make a name for herself with yarn food, let's be clear. Her work and the attention it's garnered happened purely by accident. Her sole intention had been to make fun of the high-class world of gallery art and enjoy herself.

"It started randomly," she explains. She was in bed recovering from wisdom teeth surgery when she started making mittens and got absolutely hooked. "I crocheted twelve or so pairs of them before realizing that I didn't really have a need for twelve pairs of mittens in sunny California." But the act of making the mittens had fired an inner need for her to use her hands in this way.

"Using my hands is so important to me, especially now in this time of so much phone and computers and convenience. I totally calm down in my body," she says of the handwork activity. Clare finds handwork useful in distracting her from the outside world, rooting her more firmly in the real world—defining her own time and space. "My brain gets super excited, though, and focuses on what I'm doing."

To keep the fun she'd discovered while making mittens alive, she started making sushi using yarn. Looking back on it, she thinks the transition may be due to the fact that the rice on which sushi is built is approximately the same shape and size as a mitten thumb. Coming up with this explanation, her spontaneous laugh fills the bright room. "I don't use patterns," she explains. "I can't. I didn't use a pattern with the mittens, just experimented. By the time I started the sushi, I knew how to make a thumb." Making the sushi, "I was so excited by its ridiculousness, and then I realized that the mittens were just as ridiculous as the sushi roll, really." She crafted a whole sushi plate with chopsticks, delighting herself with the work. Next a hamburger and french fries. Then a pizza slice and a grilled cheese sandwich and a whole leg of ham. It went on and on.

"Suddenly I was so excited about creating again. It bridged this strange gap that had appeared between my love for weirdly designed food and a lasting art form."

The whole transition from mittens to food was a bit weird, even for Clare. At the time, she was in a knitting bee with a wonderful knitter, Edna Hart, whose trendy boutique in Silver Lake offers knitting lessons and top quality supplies. Clare had complained to Edna, "You can make such wonderful sweaters. I can't even follow a pattern!" Edna had responded, "C'mon, you can make hamburgers!"

"And then I'd think, she's right!" Clare stops talking to laugh again. "Sometimes I think I'm possessed by a crazy little old lady who's channeling through me. How else do I know how to do this? Me: I know how to make scarves and mittens, that's it. How'd I learn to make a hamburger?"

There was more than just fun involved, she admits. For her, it was important to preserve the art form of knitting and crocheting. "Think about it: There's only, say, three good yarn stores in L.A. Is this art form going away?" she asks with alarm in her voice. "Is this art form dying? My grandmother taught me and I will always treasure that gift from her. Maybe, if I help make this kind of craft cool, it might keep people wanting to do it."

Clare's best friend is a professional photographer. The two of them hatched the plan that has led to her commercial success by making fun of the exclusivity of the art world. They photographed Clare's yarn food and printed fine-art postcards of them, the kind you can buy in museum gift shops, each listing a title for the plate of food featured and the year the work had been completed, providing Clare's contact information for art dealers. "What a hoot!" the two friends thought. So ridiculous! They arranged for the postcards to be available in local hipster shops and enjoyed their little joke. Then out of the blue, an art dealer *did* call and offered Clare a show at George's Gallery, a trendy Los Angeles art studio.

"When the gallery called, I wanted to say, 'Hey, you don't get it. I'm making fun of you! I'm not doing this to get a show. I've got this little old lady I'm channeling.'" She laughs and slaps the couch. The gallery turned out to be "pretty irreverent," Clare explains, doing cool things and not just exclusive kinds of art. "They were making art available to people and making it accessible. Their philosophy was that everyone should be able to buy some art, have art in their lives."

The show featured twenty plates of Clare's yarn food, each on a plastic wood-grain tray like the kind you see in cafeterias. She made a complete ham dinner—a huge leg of ham on the main platter with whole carrots and vegetables, and then individual dinners plates with slices of ham and a serving of vegetables on each. This ham dinner had been photographed by her production company and used as their holiday cards the previous season. She and her photographer friend even made up posters that featured the food, intimating that the work had been on exhibit at the Venice Biennial—"the hoidy toidy, most annoying show of them all."

"I was shocked by people's reactions," she tells me. "I had little old ladies' knitting clubs coming to the gallery. I had serious art-types visiting and contextualizing the work. I had little kids in there hugging the crocheted Twinkies. I felt like my work was inviting all types of people and that was so good and important to me." Plus, the work sold. Pieces she'd originally displayed in little local shops with asking prices of $40 or $50 were snatched up at the art gallery for $250 to $600. The show almost sold out opening night. Recently, Clare saw one of her pieces from that show in someone's house; she cracks up at the seriousness of it. "They had made a fancy little plexi-box for it and still had the work sitting on the wood-grain tray. It was in a place of honor."

There are countless reasons this kind of handwork appeals to Clare, not the least of which is the Zen-like quality it engenders. "It takes me out of my brain," she says. "It's tactile and it's something I can share. It exists here"—she gestures to the space in the room in front of us, defining the "real" world. "It's not like a cool conversation you had with someone. You've got something to show for it." Clare strokes her upper chest, in the area of her heart. "It's soothing. You can't think about your regular nonsense at the same time. Plus, there's the pride in having made something yourself. If someone comments on a scarf I made or a bag I'm carrying, it's like 'I made that!'" She laughs. "I made that! I didn't buy it at some cool boutique, or if it's a great meal or a baked good I cooked, I didn't buy it at the gourmet shop or a nice bakery—hey, I made it!"

Basketball, it seems, is the other, more covert reason for Clare's yarn vocation. Obsessed by the sport, she admits she watches way too much on television. "I'd think, hey, I watched eight hours of basketball this week and feel terrible about it.

What a waste of time! So I started doing this [handwork] during the games and, suddenly, watching them became okay. See, I'm doing something. I finished something. I made something."

Gesturing to the plates of food that surround us, she comments, "I did most of these during basketball games." When I ask how long a plate of food takes her to create, she calculates the time in terms of basketball games: "Two-to-three games," she says, "or I guess six to eight hours."

Clare didn't set out to make money or earn a reputation. "It was something I *had* to do. It doesn't make a lot of sense, I know." She attributes much of the attraction for this kind of handwork to the high stress of her former job. Working on music videos, commercials, pieces directed by Spike Lee and other high-profile directors, Clare was frustrated by the lack of creative participation she was granted. As the executive producer, she says, "I was the babysitter. I had to have these things"—she points to the plates of food—"or I'd have been miserable."

Each plate, she explains, now tells a story about what she'd been up to and what had been happening at the time she'd been making it. The ham dinner, for example: "I was working on a huge and horrible music video, and while flying to New York on the way to the shoot, I crocheted the ham bone. That ham bone was totally involved with the stress I was feeling about the job I was doing. It was also a way for me to keep something that I loved and was really happy about in my life while work was not so good."

Eventually, though, Clare's equilibrium got out of whack. "The job became too big," she says, "and though the company was doing all this cool, edgy stuff, the balance was off. The work was cutting into my time to make this stuff."

So she did what many a yarn-obsessed person has done before her: She quit her day job.

Clare makes her living now with the weird, quirky things that engender her contagious laugh. "I'm doing a food page for a trendy Japanese magazine, I've got this book deal, and I'm pitching a TV kids' food show. I think it's going to happen."

She knew she was on her way when others' perception of her began to change. "People knew me as this producer. They'd say, 'Hey, didn't you work on that Spike Lee number?' Now suddenly, after not producing at all—after making a point of *not* producing—people are saying to me, 'Hey, aren't you that weird crochet person?' Her grin is wider than her face. "Yes! It's starting to happen."

Recently, she was hired to teach needlework at a baby shower. "This woman, who's a trend forecaster, hired me to do it. I brought the yarn and got them started. It was instead of the traditional baby shower activity. Each person made a square and then I pieced them together to be a baby blanket." Was this shower attended by high-brow, upscale women? I ask. Grandmother types?

"No!" she hoots. "They were all young, trendy ladies." For as much as I've read in the media about the hipness of knitting, I haven't seen as much of it as I would have thought. Clare counters my experience. In her world, populated by the up-and-comers in the art and entertainment industries in Los Angeles, she's says it's the happening thing. Even high-end boutiques are offering knitting classes. One of her friends recently took a knitting class at Sues Design, a cool clothing and yarn store, and Rose McGowan (film and television actress of *Monkeybones*, *Jawbreaker*, and WB's *Charmed* fame) showed up.

If Clare's learned anything in particular from her unexpected journey, it would be that it's okay to follow pursuits that may look ridiculous to others. When she was working as a producer, taking a break to make yarn food felt silly and frivolous. "Still, it made me feel so much better. No matter how crazy people think a thing is, that's their problem." Clare reflects on the scarcity of role models for the kind of career she's chosen and how those who are interested in pursuing their own dreams often have to make their own paths. "I didn't see someone with this specific career and think 'I want that job.' I just did what I had to do."

"And you know what?" She leans closer in a conspiratorial whisper. "The world will let you do it."

A Novel Approach

The first time I saw Tara Ison, she was giving a public reading in Santa Monica, California, from her about-to-be-released first novel, *A Child Out of Alcatraz* (Faber and Faber, 1997). Dressed head to toe in off-white linen, a stunning linen duster topping off the outfit, she appeared the epitome of a stylish Los Angeles writer. She strode to the podium to read, exuding a sense of competence, boldness, and wit. I found later that her writing was as impressive as her physical presence. She seemed like someone I'd like to know better.

Sometime later I was raving to a good friend of mine, another writer, about how impressed I'd been by Tara's work.

"I *know* her," the friend informed me, telling of how the two of them had met at a graduate writing program on the East Coast, where my friend occasionally taught. When she and Tara learned they shared Los Angeles as a home port, they'd swapped phone numbers and stayed in touch. "Why don't I set up a dinner so you can meet her?"

The three of us met at a little French place in Eagle Rock one night. I don't remember what we ate or discussed, only that from that evening on, a wonderful friendship developed—not only because Tara and I had the writing bug in common, but because Tara is also a compulsive knitter.

Tara is a thirty-seven-year-old novelist, short story writer, and former screenwriter who also teaches fiction writing at the graduate level. She is Hollywood beautiful with short and sassy blonde hair, deep olive green eyes, wonderfully defined cheekbones. Her good looks never become intimidating, though, because her intellectual curiosity and literary acumen are all-absorbing. She's smart, funny, unabashed, and kind. She's also one of the toughest editors I know—we swap work with each other now and again for early feedback.

I meet with Tara on a cool Friday morning in early October to discuss knitting and creativity. She invited me over for the day to go swimming, which we never do because fall has picked this day to eclipse summer and neither of us are in the mood to get wet. We'd rather sit, chat, and knit. "I want to make you lunch," she'd said when we'd made the plans. "I can't believe I've never cooked for you."

The terrorist attacks on New York and the Pentagon are still wreaking havoc on my emotional life and I think Tara, being the perceptive, kind friend she is, has decided I need a little pampering. I'm more than glad to accept it from her.

We settle down for a morning of knitting and talking. Tara's working on a little short sweater she saw in *Vogue Knitting* and is having trouble sorting out the finishing. We read the directions and come up with ideas about what the instructions might mean, not quite sure if we're understanding the pattern or not. I'm knitting an unscripted pullover vest for my father that is starting to look a bit too big around.

"I remember my mother telling me stories about when she used to knit," Tara explains after I ask about her knitting genesis. Her mother made socks for a high school boyfriend who then put his foot right through the toe. "She never knit again," she says. A friend of her mother's taught Tara the basic knit stitch but not how to cast on or off, how to follow a pattern, or actually make things "other than those long tubelike scarves." In high school, Tara taught her best friend to knit. That friend went off to college and returned the first holiday "with these mind-boggling cable-knit, multicolored sweaters." The friend returned the favor by showing Tara how to read and follow a pattern.

Southern California, though, was too warm to wear big, gorgeous sweaters very long, Tara laments. It was when she spent a college year living in Grenoble in the French Alps that knitting and her lifestyle came together. "At the time, the mid-1980s, European women seemed to knit much more than American women, so there seemed to be many more yarn stores and a much greater variety in patterns, yarns, and supplies. Beautiful natural fiber yarns—not just the Super Yarn Mart kind of thing." And the French Alps: "That was definitely sweater weather. I made so many fantastic sweaters."

Tara's career trajectory reads like a dream. Two months after graduating from UCLA with a degree in English, she and her then-writing partner sold their first script. Unlike many scripts that are bought in Hollywood, this one was actually made into a feature film, *Don't Tell Mom the Babysitter's Dead*. From that start, Tara entered the highly paid world of film and television screenwriting, a fantasyland she inhabited for the next eight years without ever feeling that she'd found her place. "I was pleased with the excitement of it all, the money, the glamour, the lifestyle. I loved not having to go to an office every day. It was like playtime. I'd meet up with my writing partner, we'd work for a few hours, hang out, have fun." Eventually, though, Tara realized what was missing.

"Screenwriting," she says, "was at odds with the kind of expression I craved as a writer. I was proud of my overall success, but in my heart, I didn't find *that* expression of my work as a writer satisfying."

Tara took the highly unusual sidestep into novel writing. The path was difficult, money scarce, and the work hard, but she kept at it, publishing her first novel in 1997. The process was scary, but it ultimately provided the creative and psychic reward she'd been looking for. "In a way, it was like starting over in a new career. Yes, it was still writing, but I didn't have a lot of experience writing fiction. The first novel I wrote was the first real piece of fiction I'd ever done. In a way, I was more comfortable with writing screenplays; I knew the formula. Fiction writing was a whole different thing."

She's very happy, now that she's on the other side, to have made the transition. In novel writing, she's found the format in which she can explore the lives of her characters with greater introspection and linguistic complexity.

Knitting and writing go hand in hand for Tara. "My professional life as a writer is a life of the mind. But knitting is a bodily, sensual, tactile experience," she explains. "Knitting offers an escape from a writer's mind gone crazy and overwhelmed with words, sentences, language, story, character. Even if I'm thinking about my work while I knit, it's almost as if the yarn, or the cloth I'm creating, absorbs some of the extra tension, the interior white noise—which frees me up to focus."

Knitting is a key to Tara's creative process. "It's a great respite. Sometimes I put in twelve-hour days. Numerous times throughout the day, I'll literally have a sudden need to go to the couch and knit for half an hour. Like someone else might take a cigarette break. When I feel my body physically choking up, and I *need* to get out of my chair. Or when I hit a place in the work where things are snarled, then I need to work with something that isn't snarled," she says. "If I hit a knot in the work, then I knit, trying to shut out thoughts of the problem. Working with my hands, plying a yarn that's not knotted, I don't consciously try to think of ways to undo the writing knots. But after about twenty minutes of knitting, I'm able to go back to the work. I then find that my consciousness has done a lot of the work for me."

Knitting is also a form of self-empowerment for Tara. She uses a story to illustrate: "I once knit a sweater for a guy I was involved with, but we broke up before it was finished." The man hadn't seen the sweater in progress and didn't know it had been intended for him. "We stayed good friends although I pined for him for years afterward. I went ahead and finished the sweater and actually made a point of wearing it myself when we'd hang out together. He'd always compliment me on it, and I'd always think, 'Hey, you could have had this sweater!' Wearing it myself (and I still do—this was more than ten years ago) always makes me feel strong."

Where and how does knitting fit into her life now? "The word 'compulsion' comes to mind," she answers. "That sense of not wanting or being able to put something down. I'd rather knit than do so many other things." Though Tara can't say for sure when this reaction kicked in, she thinks it was there from early on, when she first realized she could actually take a big pile of string and make something out of it. "That feeling of creation," she explains, "but also the tactile sensation—literally 'hands-on.' And the pleasure of being able to wear, parade around in something you've made yourself." Knitting for other people is another a joy. "Being able to give something you've made yourself as a gift is a huge thing. Making a baby present or an afghan for someone you care about—that's time so well spent. It's a tangible love."

Trying on the unfinished tiny *Vogue* sweater we're hoping to figure out today, her face puckers in disgust. I can see she's got that perfectionist thing going. When she knits for someone else, she tells me, she's even more fussy. "I recently ripped out an afghan intended as a gift—twice. In my heart, I just didn't love the pattern. Maybe the person I'm giving it to wouldn't have cared less, but it's hard to invest in knitting something I don't love. Again, it's also hard when you've made something for someone and it doesn't fit," she gestures to the pullover vest I'm struggling with regarding size, "or hey—the person doesn't like it."

On the flip side, she tells of making a fisherman sweater for her father several years ago. "He wore it constantly. Every time I saw it on him, I wanted to cry, it made me so happy that he liked it." Her voice is reverential for a moment.

"But it doesn't always work out that way," she warns. "Sometimes the process *is* more important than the garment."

The Curative Power of Repetition

Nietzchka Keene is a forty-five-year-old filmmaker living in Madison, Wisconsin, where she teaches video-making, editing, and screenwriting to undergraduates at the university. Nietzchka creates feature-length narrative films and is currently preparing to shoot her newest script, *Barefoot to Jerusalem,* this summer.

Nietzchka describes the venture for me. "It's about a young woman, Mara, whose childhood friend commits suicide over her. He's in love with her and takes this action out of love." Though the suicide is not Mara's fault, she can't come to terms with it. One night, she walks barefoot north toward Lake Superior. She stops talking altogether and meets the devil, who tempts her with images of sainthood. "It's a modern-day devil," she explains, "a cute, young blonde Wisconsin boy, corn-fed. Not a dark, folkloric demon." Throughout her battle with the devil, Mara still won't speak. She needs the obsessive movement of walking onward to keep her going. She needs to perform some act of penance, but the devil wants to interfere with her penance and stop her from freeing her soul.

The process of shooting the film, Nietzchka explains, will be a form of hell, but a fun hell. It's great when it goes well, she says, but there are always personality issues, and how could there not be: "We're working with twenty people and filming over four weeks!" Before the actual process of filming, she's occupied with a bunch of problem-solving because once the filming starts, "it's all you can do."

Editing the film, though, is very solitary and one of the phases of filmmaking she most loves. "The shoot's over, the anxieties are over, it's now about making it work, how to weave it all together." Though the script she's written is her first guide, Nietzchka says that when it's time to start editing, she must throw out the original script and look at the material again, as if it's another form of raw material, and then shape it into a new form. That process, she says, "takes every single part of you at some point."

Nietzchka also knits. She uses the craft as a way of working on her filmmaking without actively working on it. She explains: "On days when I don't accomplish a lot, I like to sit down and knit. I don't like to actively think about the plot and questions I have, but rather, I let things percolate and allow the answers to rise." In the percolation process, she gives the knitting all her physical attention, but has to be careful not to do it too late at night or she won't be getting any sleep. "It's very involving. When I'm knitting, I can put other things aside because the knitting is so pleasurable. There's an ebb and flow to it, some kind of obsessive motion." Nietzchka sees parallels between her knitting and the script she's preparing for production. "The script is about obsessive motion, about walking, walking, carrying things, being drugged by it. It's an altered state. A curative way of repetition. The knitting is the same for me. Not much of the brain is involved, yet the body can get so into it."

Nietzchka has to be careful not to allow knitting's obsessive nature to overtake her. When she was in her late teens, she tells me, living in Massachusetts and knitting for money, she'd stay up until three or four in the morning to keep knitting. "I couldn't stop." One time, she knit for twenty-three hours straight and completed an entire sweater. "I didn't even sleep." She has to be careful she doesn't "do it for weeks on end without eating."

Knitting offers such a removal from everything else she's doing. "But you're still doing something, you're making progress."

For Nietzchka, "it's not the accomplishment" that matters, but the progress. "I don't know what it is about the motion, but the repeating, the repeating, the body takes over, you're not thinking about the motion, you're just doing it, on autopilot. There is a form of meditation in that." She pauses a moment. "If I'm anxious, I don't like knitting."

Nietzchka's grandmother owned a yarn store in a coastal resort town in Maine, and she learned the craft from her sister when she was four. By age nine, she was knitting sweaters for herself. "I always had knitting going." Her stash was supplied by her grandmother who sent her leftover yarn as birthday presents. "By the time I was in junior high school, I was doing Irish knitting that I sold to family and friends. I was thirteen, maybe fourteen. My grandmother got wind of what I was doing and asked if I'd like to knit for her store." Nietzchka asked how much she'd be paid. When her grandmother offered her ten dollars, she decided it was not worth it for her. She speaks of her grandmother with rancor. "She had these little old ladies terrorized into doing baby sweaters for a dollar," Nietzchka tells me. "Occasionally, I'd go with her to pick them up and the ladies were terrified by her. She was very successful, though."

Nietzchka's own knitting history was hit and miss for a number of years until she lived in Iceland for a year and discovered beautiful yarns. "The yarn stores in Europe had the most gorgeous Italian, French, and Dutch fibers. Rayon and linen yarns." When she moved to Wisconsin, she picked up a sweater she'd made in Iceland, the sleeves of which had never satisfied her, and started up again. She joined a knitting group that had been started by a textile artist she knew and has been at it ever since. "We compare fibers and patterns. One woman is an amazing knitter who retired as the curator of a textile museum." The group knits and yaks, finding in their camaraderie "a really specific thing." She explains: "In everyday life, we don't go around comparing fibers and patterns, and I love doing that. It's an amazingly tactile thing. Partly, I like the group for the sense of community and also for new ideas I gain about knitting."

It's the planning stages of a knitting project in which Nietzchka takes the most pleasure, and as she talks about it, the process sounds rather like the film editing she so loves. "I just start doing," she says, "working with major color variations. My mother always worked with one color and an accent of another. I leap into color." She has taken much from Kaffe Fassett's work, she says, but often ignores his color scheme. "I love to select the yarn. For this one project, a kilim, I needed twenty-one different colors." Choosing those colors was so involving and so enjoyable. While completing that project, she fell in love with playing among color and texture. The project is now finished and Nietzchka says she still hasn't worn the finished piece. "I don't care about wearing it. The satisfaction was in seeing the colors together." For her, the project has "got to be difficult or I don't enjoy it."

Because the filmmaking, like the knitting, uses up so much of her creative energies, Nietzchka says that when she begins shooting this summer, she'll have to deny herself the knitting. "I become completely fixated," she says of her creative endeavors. "The same with the garden. Anything I can get into—designing, creating patterns, selecting colors, how to work it out—I could obsess about a hat!" This is the same as the filmmaking drive, she explains. "I have to get into the obsession, spin around and around and around within it." If she lets the knitting intrude, she can't think clearly about the filmmaking. But once the film's done, she'll be back to her old standby.

"There is something that happens when I start putting colors and textures together," she says. "Imaging, picturing, looking through pattern books. It's very similar to my other creative needs. I don't know how to describe the rush of pleasure. There is something that is just—I don't know what it is—but it's like when a scene works. You know you've got it. It's a rush of love."

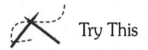 Try This

Make weird shapes and see what you come up with. Try mittens from a pattern first if that helps you envision different shapes, then create your own plates of taquitos or egg rolls, caterpillars or trees, or whatever your fancy. Have fun with your knitting and see what you can make.

chapter seven

Wise Heart

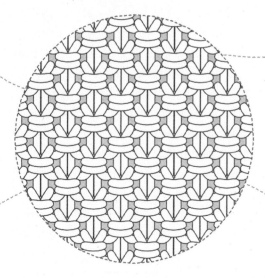

Moss Stitch
(also known as Rice Stitch)

Makes a wonderful, simple pattern—bumpy and full of texture. Nice to show off high-quality wool. The number of stitches on your needle must be even (divisible by 2) for this stitch to work properly.

Row 1: knit 1, purl 1—repeat this sequence all the way across.
Row 2: knit 1, purl 1—repeat this sequence all the way across. Texture arises out of knitting into the purl stitches and purling into the knit stitches.

Sister Elizabeth

Are knitters wiser than the average person? I wouldn't like to make that claim and have to back it up. I've met a number of knitters who seem to have no more wisdom than any other human I've run into, and I, for one, don't feel particularly sagacious as a result of my knitting. I have, though, noticed that I tend not to rush to judgment about any situation when I've got knitting in my hands. Moving slowly with the needles and yarn seems to demand a similar consideration in my own reactions to injustice, injury, and difficult situations.

I've also met quite a few longtime knitters who, by virtue of having sat still for so much of their lives and quietly reflected on what has gone on around them, have developed a degree of acceptance, tolerance, and an abiding wisdom that I admire and would like to develop in my own life. These are a few of the wonderful, wise knitters I've encountered. I'm sure there are many in your neighborhood, as well as wise teachers and sculptors, crossing guards and shop keepers, carpenters and social workers. Listen with your heart when they talk and you'll uncover them.

Sr. Elizabeth, OSF, is a Roman Catholic sister who belongs to the Franciscan Missionary Sisters for Africa and has served in Africa providing education, training, and social-work care in various countries throughout Southern and Middle Africa since the 1950s. She is also my father's sister, my aunt. As a child, long before I ever laid eyes on her, I was constantly aware of her and her work. My family gathered every evening at seven to kneel before a small shrine my parents had created above the dining-room mantelpiece and pray. This familiar family liturgy included a plea for Auntie Betty and the services she was providing in Africa. I didn't meet Auntie Betty until I was in my late teens, but when I did, I felt an immediate affinity. She's smart, compassionate, and willing to argue with or question things that others might take for granted.

She's known in public as Sr. Elizabeth, and though it feels odd in my mouth to call her such—she's always been Auntie Betty to me—I'll use her formal name here, keeping in mind her identity in the larger world. Sr. Elizabeth, like the rest of my extended family, was born in Ireland. After serving more than half a century ministering in Africa, she's now in her seventies and had been on leave in Ireland for the past few months, resting and awaiting news of her next assignment. She's just arrived in Los Angeles to celebrate my father's—her brother's—eightieth birthday. While she's here, we'll spend time together and talk about our usual topics: God and social justice, family issues and world problems, and of course knitting. Sr. Elizabeth has been knitting most of her life, and though Africa might seem an odd place to practice this craft, she's continued to do so all these years.

Sr. Elizabeth is very fair skinned, so light, in fact, her complexion looks to be made of vellum. Blue veins are visible in pale arms and legs, giving the false impression of fragility. A bounce of white hair that in years past was tucked under a brown Franciscan veil now settles like a cloud on her head. She doesn't wear a habit these days, just a simple wooden cross, and when I picked her up at the airport, I saw her wearing slacks for the first time I can recall. Judging from her vigor and compassion, the seventies are a vibrant, robust decade.

Sr. Elizabeth's openness to the way other people see the world has always struck me. She shows great respect for different beliefs, different attitudes, and vastly different ways of living life. I found this point of view encouraging when I first met her because I was struggling with my own issues surrounding Catholicism and what I interpreted as the Church's spiritual hubris, as well as its intolerance of any practice or belief deemed "other."

Yet at the same time, Sr. Elizabeth's openness does not make her own convictions wishy-washy or limp. She believes very strongly in her work, has forceful opinions about just about any subject that she'll share if asked, and isn't afraid to upset the boat to get her point across. Yet the key is "if she's asked." If she isn't, she observes quietly, patiently, not waiting to jump in and give the world a piece of her mind, but just allowing life to unfold around her and finding blessings hidden in pedestrian affairs. I don't see this as an attribute of the "quiet, weaker sex" mentality, but a type of wisdom, coupled with peace and conviction, that doesn't have to prove itself or take on others to assert its truth.

This quiet strength, in particular, is an attribute I admire.

First, let me tell you about her work so there's a context for her stories of knitting. The group of sisters to which she belongs began their work in Uganda in 1903 in answer to pleas for help. Once there, the sisters realized there was a huge need to help especially the women in the area, and they did so by opening schools, college, clinics, and hospitals. The sisters who came were doctors, nurses, nurse tutors, social workers, and educators. Sr. Elizabeth began her service in Africa in Uganda, teaching at the grade school and high school levels, as well as training teachers in the area. She lived in Uganda during Idi Amin's rule. "Between 1971 and 1979 there was a period of terror," she says, characteristically hinting at the horror of those bloodstained years without going into details. In 1980, Sr. Elizabeth was reassigned to Zimbabwe, "the former Rhodesia," she points out, which was "about to get its independence." Sr. Elizabeth with her fellow sisters worked in schools, hospitals, and in social work. "I marvel at how forgiving the people were, considering how the white regime treated them," she says of the government that controlled the country prior to Robert Mugabe's rise to power. "It was an apartheid," she explains, "though on a smaller scale to that in South Africa."

At one point, the mission station where Sr. Elizabeth lived was attacked in retaliation for giving medical supplies to the guerilla fighters. "Grenades were thrown in," she explains, "two people died and we all had to run for our lives. When we returned the next day, we found the hospital vandalized and the operating theater destroyed." Yet caring for the wounded— "anyone who presented themselves for help or medical attention was to be given it," she says—is part of the job.

In 1995, Sr. Elizabeth was assigned to South Africa. "It was just after Nelson Mandela had been released from prison, followed then by liberation from the apartheid system. It was a wonderful time to be there, to be part of the building up of the psyche of the black people. Unfortunately, you can change laws, but laws don't change attitudes." Sr. Elizabeth worked with AIDS orphans and set up an educational center for young people who had been unable to finish high school for political reasons. She also worked in literacy classes for adults, as well as a Rural Women's Association, where she taught women to cultivate gardens by getting help to drill for water. "Now that station, which was once a desert, is flourishing with greens and vegetables," she says. In each of her assignments, she strives to work herself out of a job and then move on, leaving each community self-sufficient.

Most recently, Sr. Elizabeth has been posted in Kenya, working to alleviate the devastating effects of poverty and the breakdown of the family and cultural system as a result of the AIDS pandemic. Her ministry includes providing food, emotional support, shelter, and basic education to AIDS orphans—children orphaned when their AIDS-afflicted parents die. These children, she says, may live with their grandparents for a spell, but by the time they reach six or seven years of age, they run away to fend for themselves. She tells of a sister who explained to a young boy the likely consequences of sniffing glue, and his reply: "I sniff glue because then I don't feel the pain of hunger."

Sr. Elizabeth and I, along with my sister Sheila, are sitting in Sheila's backyard watching Sheila's four young, exceedingly healthy children climb on swing sets, monkey bars, and in and out of their custom treehouse. "What is it like?" Sheila asks Sr.

Elizabeth. Sheila and I both have trouble fully picturing and understanding her life: There's no electricity, no air conditioning, no proper roads. Malnutrition, the devastation of AIDS, and poverty are rampant. "How can you look at my healthy children, my lifestyle that's so cushy in comparison, and not feel resentful for all the suffering that goes on in the world?"

Sr. Elizabeth offers a wan smile. "You do what you can do and try to let go," she says simply. She is glad, she tells us, that there *are* places like this backyard where children are healthy and well fed and don't know the pains of that life.

"If I let it all get to me," she says, "my heart would be too broken to continue the work."

Knitting Across the Nations

On our last morning together, Sr. Elizabeth and I get up at dawn and have a cup of tea. Her bags are packed and settled by the front door. She'll be leaving in perhaps an hour and I don't know that I'll ever see her again. We spend this quiet time—the kids asleep, the house quiet, and birds making almost as much noise as the nearby traffic—talking about knitting.

"I remember during the war—World War II—when I was about ten," she says. "You couldn't buy the things you needed, you couldn't even buy wool. All that was available was unwashed and unevenly spun. You'd get some nice thin parts, nice threads, and then this big clump part. But if you washed it, the wool could be nice. It was thick and then thin and very oily, but it was the only kind available—straight from the sheep."

Her memories of that time, she tells me, have more to do with her mother's knitting and what it said about their lives. "My mother knit everything for me. My pants [underwear], my stockings. We'd have an undergarment like a vest, but longer, almost a slip. She'd make all of it with lots of openwork. It was very warm."

Sr. Elizabeth says she remembers vividly being about ten and going for a medical examination in school. "I remember standing there for the doctor in my pants [underwear] and him giving me a pat on the bum, saying 'you have a good mother who looks after you' when he saw my warm hand-knit underwear."

In that time and place, she tells me, almost everything was hand-knit. "We knit our own stockings; there were no pantyhose then, of course." The women of England knit for the troops: "Socks and jumpers [pullover sweaters], mostly."

Sr. Elizabeth's mother was a fine seamstress as well as knitter. "My mother made all my clothes until the day I entered [the convent] at eighteen years of age. They had to," she says of the women of that time, and then recants. "Well, I guess she didn't *have* to. It was *her* thing. It was what she did and she was very good at it." Her voice softens. "It was what she did to raise money for the family when my dad disappeared."

Sr. Elizabeth used to knit as a young girl to earn money. "I'd knit for my neighbors. I'd charge 6 pence an ounce, so a 12-ounce ball of wool would go for 12 shillings. Of course, you couldn't buy 'balls' of wool; they came in hanks then and you'd have to unwind the hank and roll your own ball."

Many knitters were apprenticed in the craft not to their own mothers—even if, like Sr. Elizabeth, their mothers were master knitters—but to other important women in their lives. Though she learned the basics from her mother, her neighbor's mother was her primary teacher. "My neighbor and I would sit in her front room with her mother," she tells me, "and her mother would always be there to help us when we messed up."

When she joined the convent, went through her training, and initially began her mission work, Sr. Elizabeth didn't knit at all. After years of hard work, she went on a sabbatical, back home to Ireland for a rest, where a friend who knitted inspired her to start again. "I was probably in my forties. We'd sit by the fire and she was a great knitter. . . . [She] helped me with any complicated stitches and taught me. I learned to read patterns for the first time." Sr. Elizabeth quickly learned to alter patterns for economy. "Maybe I change the stitches," she explains, "to, say, two purl, two plain across the front if I don't have enough wool. I change patterns and make up my own patterns. I have to make do." She can change a written pattern to fit whatever materials are available, which, she tells me, in Africa isn't much.

She sees parallels between her handcrafts and those of the women to whom she ministers in Africa. The women in countries that have a cold season, like South Africa and Zimbabwe, knit and crochet.

The African women often knit things for the babies, she explains. "The babies would have bonnets and shawls and whole sets of matching clothing that had been knit. The babies were almost smothered in knitwear! But that's the mother's pride. It's very important to them."

She explained that for professional women, a settee can be a great point of pride. To decorate these hard-earned signs of prosperity, the women knit or crochet embellishments. "Everything in the house would have some kind of knit or crochet cover on it. The settee arms and back, the nested coffee tables. Sure, for the dust, but also as a symbol of their pride, how far they'd come."

Knitting for Her Soul

Knitting helps Sr. Elizabeth reverse the effects of her job. "I think knitting is a great gift," she says. "It has a calming effect. . . . The attention I have to pay to complicated patterns takes my mind completely off my work and restores a sense of calmness and peace. I find it soothing."

She said that friends and fellow sisters often tell her that knitting as she does would drive them mad. But when they ask her to make something as a gift, say for a newly arriving sister or someone's expected baby, Sr. Elizabeth takes the opportunity to teach them how and suggests lessons—exemplifying the "teach a man to fish" attitude she takes towards her work. "One friend in particular used to be totally aggravated by my knitting. 'How can you stand to do that?' she'd ask me. Right now, a total conversion has taken place because she's doing it on her own." Her smile, over the cup of tea, is huge; a flush of pink stains her cheeks.

The idea of empowerment that I hear so often from knitters is a source of enrichment for the lives of all who knit. It's primal and powerful to be able to make what we need for ourselves, to clothe ourselves and the ones we love.

Sr. Elizabeth also values the creative side of knitting and making her own patterns. She says she likes the challenge of attempting different designs and feels great pleasure when she understands a design well enough to do it without effort or without having to refer to instructions.

Sr. Elizabeth elucidates the wisdom she's been able to find in knitting. "I find I can't leave a mistake. I have to go back and rip no matter how far back and do it over again. Again, my friend thinks I'm crazy when she sees me doing this. 'No one will notice that,' she tells me. My answer is 'but I do.' I often think that if I could undo mistakes that I've made in life as easily, it would just be wonderful."

Sr. Elizabeth cherishes both the process of knitting and the finished garment. "The knitted garment is a special gift, and to be able to produce that from my activity is important." But she uses the activity "as a kind of mantra of praise and love."

Knitting is reflective time, she says. "I think over many things as I knit. This can be a spiritual activity, or it can just be. In religious terms, I'd call this the sacrament of the present moment." Partaking in that sacrament doesn't require any special meditative technique or even a specific intention, just doing it is enough. "Knitting can teach us the art of silence," she says, "which is so important in our day and age, in the active world we live in." Her work's demands particularly—"once people see you around, they have an impulse to approach you"—create a need for silence and escape.

Some of the aspects of Sr. Elizabeth's knitting are based on limitations that we in the West don't often think about. "Color is very important," she tells me, explaining that she prefers working with pastel shades because they suit her coloring and, more importantly, because she can see them in dusky light. "Dark colors are difficult on the eyes while knitting," she says, "especially at night. You can't see them well by candle or oil light." I'm reminded again that there's no electricity where she lives. "Pastel colors, though, you can see."

Knitting Feminism

A question recently resonated in my brain all week. An interviewer for a national magazine wanted to know if I thought the resurgence of knitting could be considered a form of backlash against feminism. Were women re-embracing domestic arts now that the promises of feminism hadn't all come true? the interviewer wanted to know. Did this trend show that a woman's place, instinctively, was tending home and hearth?

Sure, women are now a greater force to be reckoned with in the workplace, but women's wages continue to pale in comparison to men's. The glass ceiling remains in place, keeping many women from reaching positions of power within much of corporate America. On the homefront, though men may be helping out more with childcare, it's frequently the woman who takes time off work to care for a sick child, who handles most of the family's doctor visits, who's expected to participate in the PTA. After trying to have it all for the past few generations, have some women, particularly those embracing knitting, just thrown in the towel on equality and settled into their role as the little woman?

The more I thought about the question, the more I could see that the wisdom of feminism and the woman's movement is coming full circle. Every form of balanced living must embrace divergent aspects of life. All work and no play make Jane a dull woman. The fact that the current generation of twenty-somethings sees clearly that feminism and equal rights can exist contemporaneously with a desire to create, to nurture, to make tangible the emotions of love and commitment— whether by knitting, gardening, cooking, or by *any* means—is a great sign. I'd go so far as to say that the very absence of questions about feminism in the minds of new knitters tells a powerful story: We know that we can use our brains, our creativity, and our strength of will to accomplish myriad things, and we acknowledge that knitting a work of art is a valid expression of who we are. Perhaps we're lending a newfound dignity to the home arts, a dignity that had been trampled and muddied amid the important struggle for equal rights. Or perhaps we're just beginning to learn to nurture ourselves.

I think it's of note that most of the younger women exploring knitting today are highly educated, many with graduate degrees and ambitious careers. Perhaps the women who fit the suburban stay-at-home wife/mother model were already active knitters before the craft became fashionable. Whatever the reason, the majority of new knitters I've encountered are coming from an urban sensibility that encompasses a breaking-the-mold approach to life. These urban knitters are welcoming the craft as more than a way of decorating their homes and making the man in their life feel special. They see their own knitting as an important unearthing of the creative and mystical side of themselves, as a journey in self-awareness.

Given these factors, then, I'd suggest that the upsurge in interest in knitting is anything but a backlash against feminism. It shows we've come far enough to see the inherent self-nurturing to be found in knitting and have begun to champion those things that sustain and revitalize our souls.

Wisdom Comes in Many Packages

The wisdom to hold two seemingly antithetical ideas simultaneously—knitting and feminism, for instance—comes from the great well of sagacity to be discovered in this practice. With all the knitters I interviewed, the idea that they'd gained some sort of wisdom from their craft came up time and again. Even if I didn't ask outright—what pearls of wisdom have you found from knitting?—people seemed to associate their knitting experiences with the lessons they've learned about life.

Cher Brower, for example, is a forty-four-year-old professional knitting instructor and freelance knitwear designer in

Hackettstown, New Jersey. She told me about research she'd done on the history of knitting for a seminar she was preparing. She's come to believe that knitting developed from nomadic weavers among the North African coastal plains. "As the people traveled and traded and shared their knowledge and things, weaving transformed slowly into knitting, with each group of people adapting the new skill to their own environments and the materials at hand." Cher thinks it would be fascinating to retrace family ancestors and try her hand at techniques that were indigenous to that area. "When we cast on, we are all connecting to history," she explained.

On a more personal note, Cher said that knitting has taught her a great deal about knowing where and when you have control and about letting go when you have no control. She relishes knitting for the way it gives her, if only in this one area of her life, the full power of authority. "It's the only place where I can choose to keep doing it till I get it right or say 'skip it'!"

Another lesson, she told me, is that nothing is ever as hard as you think it will be. "Even the most difficult directions can be dissected and brought to simplicity."

The process and finished product are almost of equal worth in Cher's view. "The process of knitting, I think, is more important to me although I wouldn't pursue the craft if it did not have the redeeming value of being practical." Still, she said, she doesn't limit her knitting to the practical. "Sometimes I just play with a skein or color combination to feel the texture between my fingers. I'm very tactile that way. I was always a touchy-feely kid and told to put my hands in my pockets when going into a store because it's never enough for me to see."

Candace Eisner Strick is a forty-eight-year-old professional cellist and knitwear designer, author and teacher. She says that knitting has taught her the value of time. "I travel a lot and spend lots of time in airports, in transit. I can't believe the number of people who just sit there and do nothing. I mean, how is it they keep from going crazy with boredom? I want to run up to them and put some yarn and needles in their hands." She paused. "Hands—this is the other important wisdom I have gained—you only have one pair. Be thankful for every minute you have that you can knit."

Betsy Rodman is a thirty-eight-year-old knitter living in Tomkins Cove, New York. She says knitting has taught her about handcrafts and creative imagination in the health of our soul life. "Knitting," she says, "is a wonderful metaphor for a woman's life. We create an intricate web of love and family, stories and memories. We clothe our loved ones in our love and we knit that love into every stitch of the blankets, sweaters, and caps they wear. We juggle and interweave many strands all at once." Those strands, while in progress, may seem disparate or unrelated, she said, but the unfolding of our lives reveals a beautiful pattern.

Emily Wasser is a forty-three-year-old computer engineer and programmer in Potomac, Maryland, and also the mother of four children. She says knitting maintains her sanity. "As a working mother of four kids who participate in every activity under the sun, I need all the relaxation I can get. What's more, knitting is portable, so you can do it at diving meets, soccer games, and doctor's appointments. It's something that can be picked up and put down again, so that you can do it when you only have a short snatch of time." Emily said that her most productive months as a knitter are April, May, and June, when both soccer and basketball season take place simultaneously. "I have had people who see me at both soccer and basketball games ask me if my hands start to shake and tremble if I do not get my knitting 'fix.'" One time, after she'd changed her hairstyle dramatically, a woman said she'd only recognized Emily by the knitting. The main lesson Emily's taken from her knitting: "Grab your pleasure when you can."

For me, one of the key wisdom benefits of knitting has been increased patience and the realization that every stage in life is just a stage; everything changes. When my children were preschool-aged and younger, for example, I found myself adrift in the shifting tides of mommyhood. I'm not someone who played with baby dolls as a child and dreamed of becoming a mother. I didn't baby-sit as a teenager. The whole mother-world was new and unfamiliar to me. I'm a person more at home in other realms—in a fiery debate over the esoterica of literature, say, or writing essays about cultural happenings and how they shift our self-awareness. Sitting at the park for hours on end has never been my idea of a perfect day. I could only watch a child playing in a sandbox or using Play-Doh for limited periods of time. After I'd depleted my meager stores of patience, I'd need something to do that was mine, but something that could be put down quickly should a child need my help. Thus, being able to knit during that intensely mommy-stage was a lifesaver.

The thing about knitting that gave me such joy during that young-child stage was that the knitting was the only thing in my life that I could do that would stay done. The picked-up toys would not stay picked up. The bathed children would not stay clean. The washed, folded, and put-away laundry would need to be done yet again tomorrow, as would the grocery shopping, the dishwashing, and meal-making. Ditto the working world: Pieces I wrote would, by necessity, go through editors who'd ask for changes or new information to be added or a new perspective given. Even after a piece was published, there'd always be the next day's assignment to fill. Nothing ever felt done.

But knitting is blissfully different in this respect. Once I've knit a row and done it correctly, it's going to stay just like that for a very, very long time.

And the lessons continue. When I attended graduate school, knitting helped me sort out my thoughts and organize the vast quantities of heady material. If you can hold the pattern of a complicated Aran or Fair Isle straight in your mind, it's amazing how much that organizing ability comes in handy in the rest of life.

Throughout the various stages of my life, knitting has been a tool for keeping difficulties in perspective, for centering my scattered mind, and for maintaining a degree of sanity during chaotic times. As a young single woman, later as a corporate public relations professional, then as a new mother, a graduate student, and now as a full-time writer and active working woman, knitting helps me hold in balance the rich colors and vibrancy of my life.

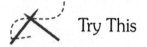 Try This

Outfit yourself with a sweater woven of self-love and care. Use the basic pattern at the back of this book, create your own pattern, or select a simple one from your local knitting shop. As you work on it, think about the wisdom you've gleaned. What has knitting taught you about patience, perseverance, and discretion, about embracing your own imperfections and those of your loved ones? How would you describe to a beginning knitter the wisdom you're unearthing, stitch by stitch?

chapter eight

Warming the Body

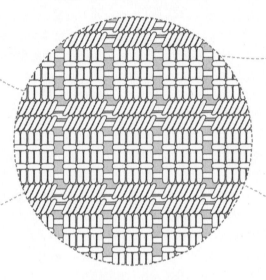

Waffle Stitch

Use over multiples of 3. Adds nice-to-the-touch texture.

Rows 1 and 3: knit 2, purl 1—repeat sequence over all
stitches.
Row 2: knit 1, purl 2—repeat sequence over all
stitches.
Row 4: knit across.

Healing Your Own Body

Clothing oneself, keeping warm on cold days, and providing for one's own physical well-being is one of the blessings of knitting. One area I hadn't considered before I began interviewing knitters, though, was the restorative power of knitting for those with catastrophic illnesses. It seems odd to me now that I didn't think of this aspect. After all, I'd come to knitting as the result of a traumatic injury and life-changing event, yet I'd given little thought to how other people might have similar experiences.

Time and again, knitters told me how knitting helped them through physical infirmities, from breast cancer and debilitating forms of fibromyalgia to cerebral palsy and brain injury. Though most didn't want to dwell on illness in these stories, it's clear that the handcraft serves a curative purpose in their lives.

Kathryn Gunn, for instance, is a fifty-one-year-old knitter in Adelaide, South Australia, who suffers from cerebral palsy. Just the fact that she learned to knit, back when she was eight years old, she said, "was something of a major feat for both me and my grandmother."

Shawn Morris, thirty-six, of Slidell, Louisiana, served as the music minister for a Catholic church in Italy for three years and is currently a catechist for Our Lady of Lourdes near New Orleans; she makes her living as a graphic artist. "About five years ago," she said, "I was very ill for over a year. If I walked across the room, I'd have to stop and take a nap. I couldn't drive because I'd fall asleep at the wheel. Knitting was my lifeline." For Shawn, "Knitting is meditation and the stitches are my mantra; it's when I'm removed from the world. I am relaxed and completely in the moment. Every stitch is also a prayer, especially when I'm knitting for someone I love." While knitting, Shawn has found that her mind becomes more focused and she's calmer. "My hands have a slight tremor, but it's unnoticeable when I'm knitting. If I go longer than a day or so without knitting, my back aches. But as soon as I start knitting, it goes away."

Many women shared stories of friends with chronic arthritis who find relief, ironically, in knitting. Regular practice gives them a mobility to their hands that is lost if they don't knit.

Cherryl Holt, fifty-one, is a social worker in Oak Park, Illinois, who found in knitting just what she needed when she underwent a partial mastectomy of her right breast. The morning after the surgery, she got out her knitting and was sitting in bed working away when the doctor came in to check her incision. "He said I should be careful about not doing a lot with my right arm, but I let him know that knitting was good exercise and did not cause any stress. So there!" Six weeks after her surgery, Cherryl started chemotherapy. "My four sessions, each three weeks apart, were hell. I was so sick and weak. I couldn't concentrate to read much, but I could do things in stockinette stitch. And that's what I did. My fingers seemed to work on their own. Just put the needles and yarn in my hands and, by reflex, I started working and also started to feel better. I believe my knitting helped me get through the chemo."

Knitters seem to want to pass on to others the blessings they've received via knitting. To this end, Cherryl's planning to knit afghans for the clinic where she underwent the chemotherapy because she was always cold while getting the treatment. The clinic has nice blankets, Cherryl said, "But it would be nicer if patients had a warm afghan made with them in mind."

Cherryl has also used knitting as art therapy in her work with women recovering from addiction. She taught them to knit as part of the recovery process. "One woman gave it up," Cherryl admitted. "She said she couldn't knit and smoke at the same time so she gave up the knitting."

Though it took illness to uncover how deeply Cherryl needed the craft as a form of meditation, she said she knew that knitting was important in her life back when she was in graduate school. "I found that knitting was a wonderful way to step back from the classroom and the internship and just to 'be.' I found I could actually solve problems while knitting. I just let my mind wander and the solution to whatever problem I was dealing with would just 'come' to me."

She eschews perfectionism, though, realizing that time and energy is too precious to spend on needless precision. "I once took a workshop from Jean Lampe and she said there are no mistakes in knitting, only design elements," Cherryl explained. "Unless the integrity of the garment is in question, the 'design element' stays."

Karen McGrath, age forty-one, lives in Ronkonkoma, New York, and was involved in two serious head-on collisions ten years ago. As a result, she suffers from migraine headaches. "The only thing that seems to help with them is when I knit," she said. "I go into my own little world and I can sometimes control the headaches." To knit during these episodes, she has to choose a project that doesn't require a pattern, something she knows off the top of her head. "The doctor said he doesn't know how it helps, but to keep on doing it."

Karen used the lesson of knitting through illness when her son was hospitalized as well. The night before the hospitalization, a member of her knitting group had asked the group to make preemie baby caps. "I was doing this while watching my son. The nurses said they could use some for the preemie unit in their hospital. It felt wonderful to be able to put my knitting talent to use."

Becky Karadin of Akron, Ohio, is forty-nine years old and suffers from fibromyalgia, a very painful, fatiguing illness that still perplexes many doctors and is often misdiagnosed. Her life has been completely circumscribed by the illness.

The first symptoms became apparent after the birth of her first child, but she thought the problems were caused by the childbirth itself. After her second child, she said, "I knew something wasn't right." She was tired all the time, completely fatigued, and in tremendous pain. Sitting was difficult; everything was difficult. "Once, after I'd gone swimming, I was so tired that I passed out on the kitchen floor." Another time, she was weeding the garden and became stuck in the crouched position. "I couldn't get up," she said. "I was calling for help, crying and laughing and unable to even roll over or move." Part of what makes this illness so frustrating, for Becky, is how little the medical community understands it.

"My doctor sent me to a rheumatologist who thought that my symptoms must all be in my head. His first words to me were 'You can't get disability for this.' That wasn't even what I was after." She continued struggling, especially when her children were small. "I had to consciously think about what I was doing to fight the fatigue," she said. Becky would have to tell herself "to put one sock on, and then another sock. And now do the kids' socks. The same with driving: Move the stick shift, push the clutch. Constant attention." Later, she was given antidepressants, yet the symptoms just got worse.

Through the pain, the fatigue, and the frustration, Becky knit. "I only have so much energy," she explained, "and time is energy. I can't stand to waste it." One of the beauties of knitting is that you can do just a few stitches here and there if that's all you've got the energy for. "When I look at a piece of knitting, I see all the stitches. I appreciate how even one stitch a day adds up. If I do one or two or ten a day, after a period of time, I'll have something. No matter how few I'm able to do at a given time, I still end up with something."

This sense of productivity saved Becky's life. There were days, she said, when she just wanted to die, so useless and unproductive did she feel. Thoughts of suicide were a constant companion. Her doctors couldn't help her. But then she realized that with her knitting she could still be a contributing member of society. Even if she could only do one stitch a day, she could do *something* useful. Thoughts of suicide left her.

Becky says that there are days when the only position she can stand to be in is lying on her back in bed. In that position, holding a book is too strenuous, as is doing much of anything. Except knitting. But no matter how limited she is on a given day, she can still feel the yarn and colors. "Even if I'm too tired to knit, I have my yarn in clear boxes that I can see from the bed and I can be designing things in my head. If it wasn't for knitting, I don't know what I would have." Her voice nearly breaks. "I don't know what I would have; everything else is just too hard."

On the positive side, Becky says she finds physical relief as well as spiritual solace while knitting. "When I'm knitting, the pain is not as overpowering. It's always there, but when I'm thinking about stitches and color and what's being made, the pain is less." These days, Becky's working with her knitting guild to make chemo caps and preemie outfits, projects that make her feel good and prove to herself that she's a contributing member of society. "No one else knows how much effort a person has to put into their life," she says thoughtfully. "Only that person and God knows." She pauses. "I know."

Healing Another

Beyond helping with physical illness, knitting has proven effective in dealing with societal ailments as well. I read an article recently about a writer, Anita Hatfield, who taught handcrafts, including knitting and crocheting, to gang members incarcerated at the Preston Youth Correctional Facility. Anita had been hired to teach the teens science, but couldn't get them to focus on the lessons. She got them sewing, knitting, quilting, and crocheting instead as a way of helping them realize that they had the power to concentrate, to learn, and to develop themselves intellectually.

The young men made outfits for premature babies. "Letters started coming in from hospitals with photos of preemies wearing our outfits," she writes. "Many of the boys were fathers already, and the sight of these babies hit home." Anita was able to use the now-proven ability of her students to concentrate in order to help them tackle the book learning. Once they could see they were capable of concentration and learning, they could—and did—apply those skills to science and other subjects.

Elizabeth Seward, the Waldorf handwork teacher and Benedictine oblate profiled in Chapter 4, has talked about teaching pregnant teens and abused women to knit. "If the women knew they had this power within them, they might then be able to see the other places in their life where they could assert their strength."

There is great power in knowing you can clothe yourself, that you can help keep others warm, that you can make what you'll need in life. This sense of inner strength cannot be under-estimated in medical, emotional, or societal terms.

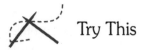 Try This

Knit as an act of healing for others. Find out from your local hospital if they need "chemo caps" (hand-knitted caps to keep warm the heads of those who've undergone chemotherapy and lost their hair) or baby blankets or baby caps. Check with your local knitting shop for patterns or search the Web—there're lots out there. Knit your thoughts of healing and wellness for the people you don't know and shower them with hand-knitted kindness.

chapter nine

Grateful Nature

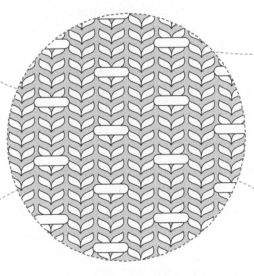

Simple Seed Stitch

This stitch adds little bobbles of texture, like tiny seeds, in recurring patterns. Work it over a number of stitches divisible by 4.

Row 1: knit 3, purl 1—repeat this sequence across all stitches.

Row 2 and all even-numbered rows: purl across.

Row 3 and 7: knit across.

Row 5: knit 1, then begin sequence to be repeated: purl 1, knit 3; continue until three stitches remain, then purl 1, knit 2.

Repeat this pattern.

Why does the craft of knitting inspire a level of gratitude and connection that other pursuits don't seem to offer? Maybe being a knitter myself skews my perspective. If I were an avid rock collector, perhaps I'd feel the same appreciation for the time I spent with a rock identification book and a handful of specimens as I feel for my knitting. I don't know. But it seems to me that most people who knit are deeply connected to that activity, they feel a sense of gratitude for this skill, and they hold strong opinions on every issue having to do with knitting: natural fibers vs. synthetics, bamboo vs. steel needles, knitting in the round vs. flat knitting, and so on. In other words, knitters feel passionately about their craft. I guess one would have to feel passionately in order to spend the amount of time it takes to make a beautiful sweater, a pair of socks, or a pair of mittens. But we do. And instead of believing the time spent knitting has been squandered or otherwise lost, when we hold in our hands the garment we've made and feel its intricate twining and intrinsic beauty, we see manifest the physical proof of time well spent.

Lizbeth Upitis takes this concept of passion, connection, and obscene investment of time to its furthest limits. One of the founding contributors at *Knitters Magazine*, she went on to be an associate editor for that publication and was later profiled in Melanie Falick's wonderful book *Knitting in America*. Lizbeth has become a world-recognized expert in the art of knitting Latvian mittens. Just the thought of a person choosing to specialize in mittens—specifically Latvian mittens even—I'm struck again by how fervent knitters are about their work.

I've never taken the time to learn a form of knitting as detailed and difficult as Latvian mittens. They're made on tiny 0 and 1 sized needles, with incredibly detailed patterns and designs that go back generations. Who, I wonder, in this day and age would spend the time to make such impractical things?

Offering Abundance That Abundance Might Be Returned

I'm sitting in the Vroman's Museum Collection shop in Pasadena on a Friday evening to find out the answer to that question. An adjunct store to the main Vroman's Book Store, the beautiful museum shop is playing host to Lizbeth Upitis and her lecture on Latvian mittens. I've arrived with just minutes to spare, certain that seating shouldn't be an issue. How many people would be willing to give up their Friday night to sit in this shop, adorable though it may be, and learn about a time-worn tradition that has little to do with life in Southern California in the new millennium?

Plenty, it turns out, and I'm just able to grab one of the last available seats. The room is filled to capacity. Many attendees are women, though there is a reasonable sprinkling of men in the audience as well. There are easily fifty to sixty people gathered, with a few kids scattered about. I check out the other women to get a demographic sense of the people interested in this kind of esoteric knitting. Many look to be in their mid to late forties; there are quite a few pairs of Birkenstocks, clogs, and sandals with heavy woolen socks. A few of the women sport colorful hand-knit vests; others wear hand-knit sweaters punctuated with intricate textures.

A microphone and projection screen are set up. Linda Urban, the reading series coordinator, takes the microphone to introduce Lizbeth. Linda looks like she can't be out of her twenties, with gorgeous long thick brown hair and not a drop of makeup. Her confidence and demeanor, though, suggest she's probably in her thirties. Linda has written about knitting books in the Vroman's newsletter and received a strong response from local people who wanted more of the same. Now she's arranged a handcraft night at the main bookstore where women meet twice a month to knit or work on other hand arts. Following up on that success, she's arranged to have Lizbeth come here from Wisconsin to give a weekend-long seminar on making Latvian mittens. Tonight's lecture is open to the public, but tomorrow the serious knitters will gather with these oh-so-thin needles and fine yarn.

Lizbeth takes the microphone to a room of applause. She's got curly, curly white/blonde hair and is wearing a kimono-type shirt with a white turtleneck underneath and black slacks. Linda and Lizbeth have just barely made it to the lecture, having been stuck on the freeway. She takes a few deep breaths, asks for the lights to be dimmed, and begins her lecture.

She uses slides to show different variations on the intricate designs used in these mittens from the small Baltic country of Latvia. Latvian mitten design uses complex symbolism and the layering of motifs, which Lizbeth explains to us.

The people around me watch the slides entranced, some taking copious notes. Lizbeth mentions the use of natural dyes, how moss is used to make green and gold colors, and she helps us see the symbols embedded in the designs: the God symbol, the cross of crosses, and the fire-cross, which looks very similar to a swastika. She explains the long history of this contentious symbol, which originally meant well-being and prosperity. "I'd hope we could take Hitler's power away from it and give it back to the people," she says. She shows us the negative and positive images of each symbol and how they're worked subtly into the mitten designs. There seem to be endless symbols for fertility including crossed stalks of wheat, heavy and interlocked, as well as a symbol of the serpent who lives under the doorway. She tells us the myth that goes along with it, including the warning to never greet someone at the threshold of the house because the serpent's lurking there.

Lizbeth explains the link between knitting and human connection. "One of the reasons we knit," Lizbeth tells the group, "is to sit together and talk, to get close."

In Latvia, she explains, showing a particularly ornate pair, making mittens and giving mittens is interwoven with preparations for marriage; a couple of hundred pairs of mittens might be involved in a single wedding. A woman presents a pair of mittens to her intended as a sign of acceptance of his marriage proposal. The mother and father of both the bride and groom receive a pair. There are special mittens worn during the wedding, mittens to be worn when the couple shares their first meal together, mittens for all the relatives, mittens for the farm workers, orchard workers—even the cows, horses, fields, and beehives have ornamental mittens made for them as part of this symbolic ritual. "If bounty is offered in the form of these many pairs of mittens, the couple may hope that bounty will be returned in kind."

Lizbeth has the lights turned up and shows us actual pairs of hand-knit Latvian mittens. The small stitches and complex designs make clear just how mind-numbingly difficult these mittens are to produce. After she explains each, she passes them around the room. They feel imbued with history, even though the pairs I'm handling have been recently made. The sense of history alive in this moment awes me, making contact with these traditional ethnic artifacts.

As we "ooh" and "ahh" over the designs, someone asks how long it takes to make a pair. Lizbeth shows us how she puts the date of each mitten's completion on its interior side. "This one mitten I made in 1991," she says and then holds up its mate. "This one I made in 1992. Does that give you an idea?"

When the lecture is over, I make an appointment to meet Lizbeth tomorrow evening after she spends the day teaching this intricate art.

Saturday evening after dinner we meet at the home of Linda Urban, the reading series curator who has generously offered us the use of her stunning restored Craftsman house on a wide avenue in Pasadena. Classical music is playing and Lizbeth is ensconced in a rocking chair knitting, her feet snuggled in slippers and purple socks. I comment on the music when I first enter. "I gave up TV years ago," she tells me.

I sit and follow her rocking motion with my eyes as we settle into a typical "knitterly" conversation, one that meanders here and there, a sharing of the self that the knitting motion of the hands makes safe. I've been on retreats where there's a candlelit sharing time and many people open up more extensively during that darkened time than they might in full sunlight; the darkness protects. The same is true with knitting. We feel almost shielded by the craft in our hands, safe enough to risk a heartfelt genuine conversation that might have been difficult or awkward otherwise. Such is my conversation with Lizbeth, starting with talk of her divorce and living on her own in Wisconsin, the peace she's found in her life and the gratitude that seems to flow from her presence when she talks about the goodness of her life.

"I find the rhythm of knitting to be the most satisfying part," she explains. "It's definitely meditative to a degree, but a different, lesser degree than meditation."

Lizbeth has been studying *taiji quan* (a soft martial art also known as tai chi) for years, in addition to primordial sound meditation. She sees all three of these—textile work, *taiji quan,* and the sound meditation—as equal parts of the same circle. "All these things impact the spiritual life; the same spark is expressed in them all. They help us access the same spirit."

Ultimately, the goal of these practices, she explains, is to shed disturbances, tensions, "turn down the fuzz, the static of daily life and get into the quiet." Lizbeth teaches all three practices. When she tells people this, they often think the combination is a strange one, believing textile art, martial arts, and sound meditation to be completely different from each other.

Not so for Lizbeth: "They're variations on the same theme, just as the same spirit takes different forms."

Still, knitting differs, in her view, from purer forms of meditation. "When you're knitting, you're more present than with meditation. "Nondecision knitting"—just knitting and knitting without having to keep track of pattern changes—"is very similar to meditation, but still, it doesn't ground me the same."

Isn't it interesting, Lizbeth asks, that the tools of knitting provide this mental health break while fitting within the Western mentality of production, the idea that we must always be productive? She says she found her way to meditation *through* knitting. "'Idle hands are the devil's work,'" she quotes the old saying. "Meditation is a valid part of my life; it's not selfish. But it's taken me a long time to realize that."

Lizbeth's early experiences with knitting, though, were far from meditative. That kind of spiritual openness wasn't cool; it didn't fit with what she was trying to do and "it didn't fit with my husband." Later, she took some time away from her earlier work in textile arts and began knitting and studying the Latvian mittens. "Again, I was very productive, making something scholarly."

All that changed when Lizbeth met a group of Latvian women who were meeting regularly to knit. "We were getting together, having classes, and I was feeling more and more peace. There was this wonderful flow of conversation, the knitting giving us access to the personal level. I was seeing them open up to each other, watching them blossom." Through this experience, Lizbeth found a deeper and more rewarding experience with her own knitting.

"I like the connection, the line, every stitch. How they connect with each other echoes how we connect with history. There's
a web. I love the ethnographic knitting especially—it shows us our
ties to other places, other times. Every stitch is part of that web.
Every person is part of that web. Knitting is not just the act of
making a stitch, it's following those who've gone before us."

Knitting mittens, for Lizbeth, is especially satisfying because
there are so many possibilities of designs, all just to fit the shape
and size of the human hand. She holds up her hand to illustrate. "The requirements are very strict—hand size, mobility—
and yet there's no end to the possibilities. It reminds me that I
have as much choice in my life as I have in making a mitten."

She tells of a Latvian myth in which a prodigal son comes
home to see his dying father, wishing to make peace with him.
The father says to the son, "Would that life were like a mitten that
could be ripped out and done again." Lizbeth nods sagaciously.

"Knitting is so satisfying because it gives us that opportunity
to go back, a chance to re-do."

I ask her about wisdom: What has she learned from all
these years of knitting? "That a grounding takes place when
you manufacture an article," she replies. "There's a closeness to
nature; using natural fibers to produce something to be worn on
the body is a way of honoring nature and the body." The
process of really learning knitting, she says, is an immersion,
and the craft, once you fully learn it, can be used to express
yourself forever; there are so many possibilities and variations.

This ability to express one's inner self is an important aspect
of knitting. She tugs at the worry beads on her wrist and points

them out to me. "I got these in Vienna," she says, "but I saw them in the airport shop in Copenhagen, and at my local mall, and again in Dar Es Salaam—the exact same bracelet." She pauses a moment to let her words sink in. "That's one of the reasons to knit."

"Meaning . . .?" I ask.

"I've seen the same outfit in Paris, Minneapolis, and Los Angeles." In this world, Lizbeth tells me, we have more than we need—or want. "Shopping, in the last twenty years, has become our biggest entertainment, shopping and TV. When we're at work, we're bitching until we can get back to shopping or TV. We need to quiet ourselves, re-establish our ties with the world."

In the United States, we're so lucky, she tells me. "We have leisure time; we can do what we want with it. Knitting is an expression of our need to be in touch with the world." Lizbeth only works with all-natural fibers and believes strongly in this approach. "Synthetics," she says, "aren't nearly as comforting." She finds working with natural fibers, on the other hand, to be cleansing. "They don't add to the filth of the world. Plastic yarns are made from oil," she points out. "The earthiness of natural fibers is similar to gardening. It's cleaner." It feeds our spirits.

The Metaphor of Fibers

Lizbeth isn't the first of the knitters I've interviewed who mentioned the importance of natural fibers. For most self-aware knitters, those who approach the craft as more than just a hobby, the role fiber plays is a crucial element. I looked deeper into the metaphorical meaning of certain fibers and found some interesting ideas tying into spiritual principles and strongly held personal beliefs.

For instance, I learned that in Judaism, there's the concept of *'hoq*, a law based on pure faith with no explanation or logical sense to it. One such *'hoq* is the prohibition of *Sha'atnez,* a law that forbids a person from wearing a garment that is made from interweaving wool and linen. At the same time, though, this law also obligates the High Priest to wear such a garment. It seems that linen, in this concept, represents the vegetable kingdom whose sole existence is limited to sustaining and reproducing life. The wool represents the animal kingdom, which contains the spark of instinctive spirituality. Thus, a garment made of interweaving these two fibers blurs the line between the physical and spiritual and is best left, I gather, to the High Priest, whose job it is to bring together these two sides of our nature. The common Jew is not to wear these interweaving fibers because of the difficulty in reconciling these two elements; the High Priest, though, has the power to make this reconciliation.

Likewise, in Roman Catholicism, all altar clothes must be made of linen. I ask Elizabeth Seward, the Waldorf handwork teacher and Benedictine oblate of Chapter 4 about this. "Linen starts in the earth and grows, always reaching towards the sky, towards heaven," she says, pointing out the metaphorical meaning of that particular fiber. In her way of seeing things, linen represents both the earth—the physical side of our nature—and the divine. Thus, heaven and earth are united in this one fiber. She contrasts working with linen to working with animalistic wool.

Cotton, though, Elizabeth explains, "just sits there." Think about the ball of cotton growing, she suggests. It seems to hover in midair. It is the product of the plant, but it's not planted itself. "It's not rooted. It's not reaching. It's just there." Elizabeth's experience of knitting cotton reflects its nonrooted quality.

Her favorite fiber is silk, which she says "has a quality of light that makes it a joy to work with."

Prior to these investigations, I'd never given that much thought to specific fibers. I'd always noted the animal aspects of the rawer wool I'd knit, but beyond that, not much.

I've often found bits of hay or dried grass in the wool I'm knitting, which reminds me of its source. I find it harmonizing, being aware of the animal's gift to me and my using that gift to bless someone else's life. Taking the time to knit the sheep's wool, to honor its gift, to see in those bits of hay the particular life that has allowed this sweater to come into being—there's something earthy and holy about that.

Take time, when you next pick out a knitting project, to think about what the fibers mean to you. Do you care if it's natural or synthetic? Does knitting with synthetic feel like knitting plastic soda bottles? Can you distinguish on touch alone the different kinds of fibers? How can learning to tell by feel help your ability to discriminate between that which is real and that which is false in a larger sense? Interesting questions to ponder.

Our Watering Hole

L'Atelier is one of the premier knitting shops on the West Coast, a two-store operation owned by Karen Damskey and Leslie Stormon. The branch Leslie oversees perches unobtrusively on fashionable Montana Avenue in Santa Monica. Little boutiques dot the landscape, offering designer clothes—nothing you'd see at the local mall—for outrageous prices. Finding parking on Montana is an expedition in itself. The media regularly quotes Leslie and Karen about their celebrity knitting clients. They serve the high-end customers of Beverly Hills and supplied the knitting needs of Monica Lewinsky as she knit and purled her way through the Clinton impeachment hearings. It is one of the coolest places to be seen in Los Angeles these days.

I've come on a foggy March morning to see what all the fuss is about. The shop is an unassuming stucco building in a smallish minimall on the corner of Montana and Twelfth. Towers of yarn cubbies fill the shop, organized by fiber and color. There's a big counter space, like a cutting table at a fabric store, toward the back. A large table, as inviting as your best friend's kitchen, fills out the front. There's a vase stocked with knitting needles, like a flower arrangement, at the center. Here you can come in with your knitting and spend an hour or so, get help with a project you're working on, try out a new yarn, and see if there's something you'd like to make with it.

Leslie bustles around with her tape measure around her neck like a boa; her two assistants, Randi and Carol, are her extra hands. Leslie worked previously in the garment industry and can sort out any knitting problem in a flash. She appears to be in her late fifties, has a trendy blonde haircut, and leathery tanned skin. As I sit and watch, she crafts custom patterns for whoever asks her.

This is how it works: You come in with an idea or a picture of what you want to make; you find a yarn you like and take it to Leslie. She has you sit down and knit up a small swatch with the yarn you've chosen on the needles waiting in the vase on the kitchen table. While you do that, she sketches on paper what you've described: short sleeves, a low neck, raglan arms . . . whatever. When your swatch is done, she determines your gauge, writes out what you need to do where, how many inches wide, when to decrease. You leave with just the right amount of yarn, an expert's made-to-order pattern, and the confidence you need to do that project you've always wanted to try but have been too afraid to actually do. With Leslie urging you on, you know you can.

While watching the ebb and flow of the morning's activities, I chat with Carol, who's steaming knitted items that have just come back from the professional finishers. As each piece is completed, she swaddles it in tissue paper and snuggles the sweater into a stunningly beautiful box. The clients, who pay between $50 and $100 to have their handwork completed for them, will stop in later to pick their sweaters up.

"Some of them are beginning knitters and can't pick up the stitches for the neck, say," Carol explains in a thick New York accent. "Or maybe they can't do the complicated joining that a

particular sweater calls for. Or maybe they just don't like finishing." Carol pulls a thick, bulky weight jacket out of the pile
and begins steaming it. "This zipper," she points to the front of
the jacket, "might have been a problem, so our finishers do that
part." After what the clients have spent on the yarn, the investment in professional finishing is worthwhile. I touch the heavy-
gauge jacket as Carol folds it. The feeling is total luxury.

"What is this?" I ask Carol incredulously, having never felt a
yarn quite this delicious.

"Cashmere."

Everyone in the shop takes turns touching the natural,
sheep-colored jacket. It's simple in design, with huge stockingette
stitches. It wouldn't take long to make, but maybe a short lifetime to pay for. The yarn's as thick as any bulky yarn I've ever
seen, but 100 percent cashmere. I had no idea such high-end
yarns existed. That sweater alone must be worth the economy of
a small Caribbean country. No wonder its maker decided to pay
$80 to have the zipper put in rather than messing up hundreds
of dollars worth of cashmere. But then, compared with the prices
for sweaters up and down Montana, the price of these luxury
yarns aren't out of line for this neighborhood. A good sweater,
especially a custom-made one, is expensive.

Taking a quick look around, I find skeins priced between
about $9 and $60. You can get nice yarn here without going
into serious debt, but the higher-end yarns always tempt.

I sit and watch and knit from midmorning through the
lunch hour. One woman comes in with her own personal knitting expert in tow. The woman picks the yarns she wants to

work with and her personal expert gives a thumbs-up or thumbs-down on her choices. She looks utterly exotic, with long inky-black hair, dark glasses, and tiger print leggings paired with matching high-heeled thongs. She looks at yarn while talking on her cell phone, two calls at once—"Can I put you on hold?" she says to both callers while she confers with her personal expert on yarn choices. Once the committee selects the yarn, she goes back to her calls while her expert casts on stitches to make sure the yarn is right and to give her a head start on the knitting process.

The women who visit this shop are all well dressed, most leaning to the edgy side of the fashion spectrum. They talk about trips to Europe and how foot-and-mouth disease is ruining European dining options. Soon, talk turns to menopause and hormone replacement therapy. Later, a young woman in her twenties comes in wanting to make a sweater for her boyfriend. Randi won't let her do it.

"Trust me," Randi counsels the young woman, "it's the kiss of death. Now, maybe, if you were engaged . . ."

Two mid-thirties women arrive, one of whom is a dead ringer for Meg Ryan. I'm afraid to ask, lest I seem a celebrity hound. The companion tells Carol about the dream she had last night. "When I went to visit my in-laws, I got there and real-ized I'd forgotten my knitting."

"That's not a dream," Carol quips. "It's a nightmare."

The Meg Ryan look-alike is wearing a beautiful color-changing scarf. Everyone asks her how she made it, and how she blended the colors like that. She gives easy-to-follow instructions.

"This knitting shop is our watering hole," another woman tells me, meaning a gathering place.

Not all patrons have the time to hang out and chat, though. Carol says that many of their best customers are women executives who call ahead to order their yarn, pull up to the curb, rush in to pick it up, and roar off to their jobs again. On weekends, when the workweek is through, occasionally she gets to know these women. "Saturdays, the place is so packed, then, you can't move."

Wanting to Be "Mommed"

Karen Damskey oversees the second store, located in Manhattan Beach—a town where the women driving sports cars and SUVs all seem to be wearing sailing attire, have deep tans, and bank balances far above the nation's average. When I visit, Karen swings into the shop, a bundle of energy with short, blondish hair cut in a perky style and fair skin with just a hint of tan. She's dressed head-to-toe in black: short skirt, opaque tights, turtleneck sweater. We sit in the plush armchairs near the front windows of the shop; she talks quickly, bursting with intensity.

She opened the first shop with Leslie here in Manhattan Beach twenty-five years ago, she tells me, but it was then primarily a needlepoint store. "We created our own designs and graphed them onto canvases for our clients," she explains.

Then, in the late seventies, there was a huge fiber resurgence. Designer sweaters began selling in boutiques from $200, which was an unheard-of price. Up until that time, most of the yarns available in the United States were synthetics, the acrylics you'd buy at Woolworth's or K-Mart. "We started importing incredible yarns from Italy and all over Europe." (As an aside, she tells me that U.S. consumption of yarn ranks right next to tiny Belgium; that's how little yarn the United States uses.)

Over time, she and Leslie began to transfer the knowledge of design, color, and graphics they'd developed for needlepoint and apply it to knitting. They experienced success after success and the market seems to be ever-expanding.

We talk about the recent upsurge in young knitters, the hip trend. She says that knitting shops have to attract an ever-younger market to survive.

Who are these new knitters? I ask.

"Many people associate this upsurge with the idea of a baby boom—that younger knitters are knitting for new babies and that's it. I hate that," she says, vehement, leaning forward in her plush armchair. She describes the new young knitter: A hip and savvy professional woman with a high-powered career who uses knitting as a form of stress reduction and a way to be fashionable without spending $600 to $700 on designer sweaters.

I ask her about the celebrity hoopla.

"A lot of famous people are knitting now and somehow that makes the craft more valuable to certain people." She says that Monica Lewinsky's knitting during the impeachment hearings generated a lot of media interest that had a snowball effect. "We'd seen interest in knitting on the rise before that, but then the media jumped on the bandwagon. People came in wanting to learn to knit because they'd seen or read about someone they admired who knit."

Recently, she said they've seen a lot of very young knitters, sixteen to twenty years old. "They're doing accessories—scarves, bags, shawls, purses." Sweaters, it seems, looked like too big an undertaking to these very young knitters.

If it's just a trend then, I wonder, what will happen when its moment passes? In Karen's experience, there's nothing to fear. "Most people who learn to knit and begin to love it will always knit. They may stop for a time, but they invariably pick it up again."

She says that knitting seems to be in the genes. "Some people come in here to learn to knit. They've never knit before and yet they'll have a natural affinity for one particular knitting technique—the European style, American, or British. Invariably, the technique they're most comfortable with will correspond to the place their ancestors came from." She ponders this a moment.

Besides, the idea that the craft can be fashionable one minute and a passing trend the next is nothing new to Karen, who's seen the cycle before. The hot knitting celebrities today might be Julia Roberts, Hilary Swank, Brooke Shields, and the crowd from *Ally McBeal,* but "in the 1980s, it was Joan Collins and Angie Dickinson." There will always be celebrities who knit.

"People come here because of our knitting experience," she says. "We have doctors, attorneys, and high-profile career people. They're giving and working all the time and never getting personalized service, one-on-one, for their own needs. They're looking for a creative outlet, a way to relax, the whole set up."

Karen's clients may travel incredible distances and spend a great deal of money in order to buy the right yarn from her.

"Knitting isn't cheap," she explains, but it is easier than painting a picture and yet gives the same kinds of satisfaction. "You don't need to have a great color sense. We'll help you with that. You don't need a particular artistic talent to do this, yet you can still be very creative." And, she says, "Two hours of instructions is enough to get anyone going."

It's the psychotherapists and psychiatrists who really appreciate what her store offers, she tells me. "They're the ones who need the most therapy." Professionals in those fields have been listening to other people all day. "They come here or call to chat because they know they'll get someone to listen to them. Think for a moment about who would have traditionally taught people to knit: a mother, an aunt, a grandmother." In contemporary society, Karen explains, there's less mother/daughter-type female connection. "The women who come here want to be 'mommed,' they want nurturing, they want to work with others collaboratively, creatively." Some of her clients come in every day to knit and to find community. Some come a few times a week and others every month or so. "They're not employees, but they know the shop as well as we do. They'll lend a hand if needed, help someone figure out a tough knitting project. Are you wondering if you're on the right medication? Someone here will know what's best. Wondering about child-rearing, where to find a better job? Someone will know. Politics. News. Everything gets covered. It's like a bar." She smiles at her analogy. "We're the *Cheers* of knitting."

To illustrate her point she tells of a few of the women she's gotten to know through the shop. "There's a woman in Chicago who calls daily. She's dying and wants human contact. Another in North Carolina's seriously ill and calls, looking for the humanity. They came to us through our mail order business. Now they're like friends." Karen points to a woman knitting away at the counter. "That's Judy," she says conspiratorially. "She's got this high-profile job; she's in the spotlight regularly. But, really, she's really introverted. To do her job, she pulls up all that energy and does what she has to do. But then she needs a few days of knitting and quiet to come down. She finds that here."

I ask about spiritual ties.

Karen says she never noticed the spiritual aspect of knitting until she was in her early forties. Early on, when knitting was always tied to her business, Karen could only allow herself to enjoy it as a work-related project, something productive. "It was difficult to allow myself to just sit and knit. If it was a job, I could justify it, but I couldn't knit to dabble."

Karen has changed her focus, as have most of the knitters she's meeting these days. "That's the difficult thing, sometimes: getting women to just give in to the process of knitting and not focus so much on the product." She relates this to the larger issue of the women's movement. "A lot of women between forty-five and sixty were taught that they could do it all. Women's lib, entering the workforce, and so on. They think it's self-indulgent to do something simply because you want to do it. They're project-motivated, making huge commitments and trying to do everything perfectly."

How does she work with these women?

"I tell them to go look at the commercially sold hand-knit sweaters at Neiman Marcus, the ones they keep behind the counters. Very expensive. Look closely: You'll find flaws there." She tells the women that if those sweaters can sell for such outrageous prices with a few little flaws, then maybe they should allow themselves a few flaws, too. "There's a sign I refer to a lot. It says that 'less than perfect is not a sign of failure.' So many of us have the critical urge."

This, it seems, is what's bringing the women, especially the overachievers, back time and time again. "This is maybe the one place in their lives where they don't have to be perfect."

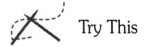 Try This

Go to a local crafts store and buy some inexpensive cotton yarn. Check the ball band—most include a pattern for making a washcloth or dishcloth. I made these as washcloths for bathtime when my children were infants and now I make them as wonderful dishcloths that are nearly indestructible. The good news: They never stink! Pair a hand-knitted washcloth with a loofah pad and some exotic soap for a special gift. There's a lot to be grateful for in small things.

chapter ten

Of a Piece

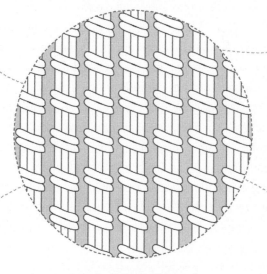

Irish Moss Stitch

This is an easy-to-do, diagonally moving version of the moss stitch. Knit it over multiples of 3.

Row 1: knit 1, purl 1—repeat sequence over all stitches.
Row 2: knit 1, purl 1, so that you knit the purl stitches and purl the knit stitches from the previous row—repeat sequence over all stitches.
Row 3: purl 1, knit 1.
Row 4: purl 1, knit 1, so that you purl the knit stitches and knit the purl stitches from the previous row—repeat sequence over all stitches.

It's two days after the World Trade Center collapse and I am unable to function. I watched yesterday, with my kids as they hoisted on their backpacks ready for the school day to begin, scenes of destruction that I am still unable to fathom; it will be months if not years, I fear, before the scope of what's happened can penetrate my mind. As the second tower imploded, live in Technicolor on our screen, my six-year-old daughter, Hope, ran to her bedroom to get her ceramic angel. The angel, which had been a baby shower gift when I was expecting her birth, used to be a nightlight, but Hope's since removed the inner working and keeps the ceramic angel as a playmate. She came back to the television set just as CNN showed the first of countless repeats of the horrific scene. Hope held her angel to the television screen so that the angel could see the destruction, confident in the belief that the angel would be there with the wounded and dying. This image continues to haunt me; I wish I could believe today as simply as Hope believes.

Later, I tell my friend Marjorie about Hope's actions. I e-mailed her because I'm as yet unable to talk with people about these happenings. Marjorie's older brother has been fighting the fires at the Pentagon, the very place where her father, as a military physician, had worked until recently. Marjorie grew up an army brat on bases around the world; she's also Arab-American.

"Hope was well named," Marjorie e-mailed back, telling me she's as stunned and incapable of normal action as I am.

I've been watching the news nearly nonstop since the attacks. When I get sick of seeing the same scenes before my eyes, I switch off the TV long enough to read every word of coverage from the *Los Angeles Times*. I can think of nothing else. It's a huge relief when the school day comes to an end and I'm forced to turn off the television and function as a mother, if only at 10 percent capacity.

As a freelance writer working for myself, I have no clocks to punch, no bosses to appease; if I wish to spend my entire day in the pain and sadness of this tragedy, I can do so. In some ways, I think of this as a blessing. It seems vitally important to me, somehow, to be a witness to these events. To *not* brush them off and get back to normal as soon as possible, but to feel as deeply as I must the heartbreak and incredible grief that swamps me. While everyone talks of retaliation and patriotism, buying flags and making God Bless America signs, I can do nothing more than feel the huge, overwhelming pain of these events.

I don't want to talk about why someone would do such a thing. I don't want to analyze what America's response should be or how our world is forever changed. To do any of those things requires an ability to intellectualize something I haven't even begun to process emotionally. Some might accuse me of morbidity, but it seems important to be present with this destruction, to feel it deeply and honestly, to recognize how badly this hurts. Only when I can fully embrace my own sense of woundedness will there be any hope of determining how to move forward.

By the second half of the second day, I can do one thing other than watch the news and read the papers. I can knit. It seems stupid to think of this craft as anything important in the light of what has occurred, but still I do. I need to center myself again. It's not fear I'm battling, though knitting is a good anti-dote to fear, but deep, abiding sadness, irreconcilable loss, the sense of things being torn asunder. A good friend of mine who's a native of Manhattan (but now an avowed Angeleno) is grieving as well. We both agree that instead of waving flags, what we feel like doing is following the Jewish rite of mourning, which involves wearing a piece of black fabric pinned to one's garment, fabric that's been rent to show the irretrievable nature of loss.

As a writer, I don't recognize this silence. I am used to making my opinions known clearly and sometimes forcefully. Today, words fail me. Two sticks and a ball of wool are my only form of communication. I know the words will return, but until they do, I'm grateful to know my knitting can say for me what I cannot say for myself. This is what my knitting tells me: that I have faith in tomorrow. That we are all joined together. That each stitch is vital to hold the garment together, just as each person is vital to this world.

So I knit. Not as a way to rejoin those rent pieces; such is far beyond me. But to remember the unity that underlies all life. Today, when I knit, each stitch represents to me the people whose lives where cut short by this tragedy. Like my time in the hospital trauma center, I can hold each soul in my thoughts for just a moment and pay a quiet kind of tribute in my knitting. It's not much, I know, but it feels important. I can look at the won-derful way the stitches hang together and acknowledge that yes, if a gash were torn into this work, huge chunks would unravel. The damage could not easily be rectified. Such is the nature of this tragedy.

And yet at the same time I realize that we need to embrace unity. Not just American unity symbolized by the red, white, and blue that has suddenly appeared on every street corner. Not just the unity of the NATO alliance and its wonderfully supportive statement that "an attack on one is an attack on all," but the unity of *all* humanity.

If we can get beyond borders and ways of creating separation—whether by ethnicity, religion, or geography—maybe we could see things clearly. We are all made of the same materials, we are all joined in the knitted garment of life. Whether terrorism tears a gaping hole in the flashy center of the fabric or economic injustice slowly eats away at a sleeve, the damage to one part of humanity is damage to the whole. We are each stitches, necessary for a completed work, holding together our neighborhoods, our communities, our states, and our nations. Unless we see and respect this joined nature of our lives, we will certainly unravel.

So I knit and I cry; and grief threatens to overwhelm me. And I try to make this piece I knit an artistic statement of what I believe. I try to celebrate the diversity of the peoples of the world the way I celebrate the diversity of yarn colors and textures, of sweater options and knitted choices. If there were only one or two types of sweaters available to me to knit, how quickly I'd be bored with those types. But there are countless. Thank God, there are countless.

I've been reading in the paper lately about how our nation's priorities seem to have shifted dramatically in the wake of September 11. Sales of board games like Scrabble and Monopoly are skyrocketing. Parents are staying home to be with their children, resurrecting fallen-by-the-wayside rituals like bedtime reading and family dinners. This one horrific event has taught us just how precious our time on Earth is and how lucky we are to have these beautiful children, spouses, friends, families. We're taking the time to cherish them. I don't know how long this reconnection phase will last, but I hope the hard-won lesson of that terrible day isn't lost in the months and years to come.

One thing I have noticed is that more people have been asking me to teach them to knit. I'm going to a women's group this coming Sunday. Twenty-five professional women want to spend a few hours with me and learn an ancient craft.

These women, like me, are not looking to turn the clock back to more "innocent" times, to an age when women feathered the nest, tending home and hearth to the exclusion of professional and interior lives.

No, we're women who are educated, who are competent, who can make our ways in the world. We want to spend time with ourselves, awake and aware, as we go. We want to relish the fruits of all our hard-won educational and professional pursuits by taking the time to sit still and count our blessings. We want to show others how much they mean to us by making a piece of ourselves for them to wear. We want to fuel that great creative urge into a productive outlet.

I read once that the opposite of war isn't peace but creation. As war begins and deaths from September 11 are tallied, as life takes on the luminance of its true precious nature, I knit. I knit to see the connection with my fellow human, to replicate in my actions the web of humanity that ties me not only to those devastated in New York, Boston, and at the Pentagon, but with all my brothers and sisters around the world. It is indeed a global community in which we live, and when I knit, I am reminded of this.

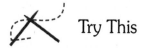 ## Try This

Design and knit your own creation. Check out a book from your local library on sweater design, or just go for it with what you know. Measure and lay out on paper what you want it to look like. Determine your gauge and plot your own creation. Wearing something you designed and knit for yourself is one of the most fulfilling acts of self-care you can do.

Appendix

How to Get Started

If you know a knitter, ask him or her to teach you. If there is a local knitting shop, stop in and spend an hour saying hi and seeing what's available. Take your time, pick up a skein of yarn. Feel it, smell it, imagine what you might like to make. Look at the hand-knit things hanging in the shop. What appeals to you: texture? Color? A particular style of design? Don't limit yourself, thinking you'd best start with a boring scarf in an ugly yarn because you're not adept yet. There's no need to start with the ugly. You *can* make something beautiful your first time out.

My six-year-old daughter started with a small bag, basically a 6- x 10-inch rectangle that she knit out of the most stunning hand-dyed wool. The colors were variegated, reflecting the blues and whites and pale purples of the sky right after the blush of dawn has left. She used large wooden needles, number 10, I think. When her rectangle was done, we sewed on a piece of silky fabric as a liner and then sewed up the sides, leaving a little flap for a button. She didn't even make a button hole, just chose a button that would fit through the existing spaces in her knitting. She made the shoulder strap by braiding the left-over yarn. It's a beautiful bag that I borrow from her on occasion.

There's no reason to think you have to settle for ugly just because you've never knit before. Pick a yarn that appeals to your sense of touch, something soft and easily manipulated in your hands. Choose only colors that excite you. Tell whoever's helping you that you want your first project to be as simple as possible but that you won't abandon your aesthetic sensibilities. Everything you make can be beautiful.

When you're selecting a beginning project, see if you can find one that utilizes just the basic garter stitch (directions given at the start of Chapter 2). Keep doing that stitch until you feel confident, until you can see what you're doing and can recognize what's a stitch and what isn't. Then pick a project that adds a purl stitch to your repertoire. Then something that uses the knit-one-side, purl-the-other-side sequence of the stockinette stitch. Little by little, add a new skill, always making sure to buy the best yarn you can and to treat your work with the respect it deserves as a hand-wrought work of art. Keep at it. Knit with friends. Find a knitting group. Hang out at the local knitting shop. Knit during lunchtime in the office. Prop open books when you go to the library to study and knit while you cram for finals. Knit on the subway or in the car (as long as someone else is driving). Knit while your kids practice soccer and go to their piano lessons. Knit while you listen to music or watch a television program. Knit as a reward. Knit as a meditative discipline. Knit as a prayer. Knit as a hobby. Knit to make a tangible something and then knit just to be in the process. Keep at it until it's as easy and thoughtless and life-sustaining as breathing.

Finding a Local Knitting Shop

The first step to finding a local knitting shop is the Yellow Pages. Look under Knitting, Yarn, and Needlework categories. Your best bet is to find a small, privately owned shop where the owner and salespeople know how to knit themselves. I'd shy away from large craft stores because most of the employees there are not knitters and may not be as helpful as the smaller boutique stores. You may pay more for your yarn, but you'll select from a vastly wider range of yarns, have access to more varieties of natural fibers, and receive expert help and guidance. If you're going to put all those hours into making that sweater, scarf, bag, or afghan, you don't want to waste that time by using cheap yarn that may pill up and will never give you the same luxurious feel of the best yarn. Even a beginning project can be a work of art if you use a high-quality yarn.

In addition to providing lessons, encouragement, and help when you get messed up, the people at your local knitting shop can sometimes create custom patterns for you, often at no charge. If you have an idea of what you want the piece to look like—a photograph or a drawing can help, but isn't always necessary—bring this idea into the shop. Explain to the expert on hand what you want to do. She (or he) may find an existing pattern that might be adjusted to fit your expectations, make suggestions on yarns that will ensure your project is as fine as possible, or may even draft out an individually designed pattern for you, taking into consideration your gauge and yarn choices.

If there are no small knitting shops near you, you may need to work a little harder to get the help and supplies you need. The Internet has a wealth of knitting sites. There are Web sites that offer instruction and helpful hints, as well as bulletin boards where you can post your current problem with a knitting project and receive advice from other knitters, and retail outlets where you can purchase patterns, needles, and all kinds of incredible yarns. Because colors don't always show up accurately on a computer monitor and texture is impossible to judge in cyber-space, it's a good idea to request a color sample card of the yarn you're considering prior to ordering. You may be charged a small fee for this, but that fee is often applicable toward sub-sequent purchases.

Learning Through Others

Though I've heard it's possible to teach yourself to knit if you have a good how-to book and copious dedication, I'm leery of this approach. It seems to me that knitting, like reading to a child, is best done in person, one-on-one, in a cozy, inviting atmosphere. If there's a person in your life who knows how to knit, take advantage of this and ask him or her to work with you. Most knitters I know are thrilled to pass on their knowledge and to get another person hooked on their own obsessive hobby.

Most knitting shops offer classes. Some charge a fee, others provide free individualized instruction as long as you purchase the supplies for your project there. Some of the world's most expert knitters work in these kinds of shops; soak up their expertise.

No matter what, don't do what I did when I returned from Ireland and had no one to turn to for knitting advice. The first time I tried to knit with double-pointed needles, for example, was a fiasco. I hated asking for help if I thought I could figure something out on my own; I'm a bit bullheaded in this way. I followed the directions for using double-pointed needles as written in the pattern and looked carefully at the picture, determined to make sense of the process. The illustration showed a pair of hands holding three small needles in a triangular shape, demonstrating how a sleeve knit in the round should be constructed and how many stitches needed to be on each of the three needles. The process looked straightforward enough, I thought, until I tried it. My package of double-pointed needles came with four needles, not the three shown in the illustration. One of the needles must be an extra, I reasoned, in case I lose one. How considerate of the needle manufacturer!

Trying to knit in the round on three double-pointed needles is virtually impossible, I soon learned. All the stitches kept bunching up on one needle until they couldn't fit and the round shape was tweaked into something it wasn't meant to be. Three days of messing with the needles and following the illustration ensued until I finally broke down and went to a knitting shop to ask for help. The women there had a good-natured laugh at my attempt and showed me how the fourth needle was used as the working needle. The process was suddenly a million times easier once someone demonstrated, in person, how to do it.

Today, many of us pride ourselves on our self-sufficiency, but in so many ways, this very trait cuts us off from the abundant wisdom and help others are willing to give us. It's as if we refuse to accept a precious gift being offered. The ability to ask for help and to graciously receive it is, in my estimation, one of the most wonderful side effects of the knitting process. It's hard to find a totally self-taught, self-sufficient knitter, and that's a good thing.

An incredible benefit of communal knitting is the fruitful, heartfelt conversation that arises organically when you knit with another human. When your hands are busy, your mind drifts easily to fascinating and sometimes very intimate conversational topics; and sharing about your life, your experience, and your hopes feels a little less terrifying when you're working on a project. You can always segue back to craft issues and discussions of yarn if the topics become too intimate.

I know of knitters who have some of the deepest conversations with each other at their regular knitting meeting. In one particular group, the ground rules are that the first half hour of the gathering, each person works on his or her own knitting silently. This gives everyone a chance to shuck off pedestrian problems. Then, thanks to the calming effects of knitting, each person slowly settles into the quiet place within. After half an hour of meditative knitting, the floor is opened to discussion and the topics that arise invariably start off from a deep place:

where a person thinks his or her life may be going. Concerns about a sick family member. Perhaps a dream deferred that's recently been calling. The resulting conversations have the soul-satisfying feel of communion about them and provide a vital psychological and psychic grounding.

There are many knitting groups and clubs across the nation. The Knitting Guild of America has its own setup of guild meetings that you can access. Or call around. Ask friends and fellow knitters. Find a group of people to support you and to whom you can lend your own support. This deep sense of belonging, which so many of us resist in favor of the hollow idea of self-sufficiency, is one of the greatest gifts available to members of the human race.

Basic Get-Going Pattern

This is a very easy-to-complete sweater I created after seeing similar ones at outrageous prices (considering the simplicity of the design and materials) at local boutiques. I've written the pattern to be done in the round. If you're a beginning knitter, find someone to help you with the directions. If you've done a pattern before and are familiar with working in the round, this should be a walk in the park.

Sleeveless Rolled Neck Pullover

Knitting in the Round

To knit in the round, you use needles connected by a cord of plastic to create a large, connected oval knitted piece. Remember those spool knitters you used as a child that made endless snakes? This method uses a large snake-type construction to make a tube shape, to which arm holes and sleeves may be added. This means you don't have to sew up side seams afterwards.

The other advantage of knitting in the round is that you get to knit every row to achieve a stockinette stitch—as opposed to knit one row, purl one row, which you'd do if you were using straight needles. With straight needles, every other row is done on the back side of the work. With knitting in the round, you're always working on the front side of the work, hence, no need to reverse your stitches. If you've never done it before, buy a pair of needles and experiment. Once you get the hang of it, you may never go back to knitting with straight needles (also known as "flat" or "piece" knitting) again.

Size 36 (38)
Directions in parentheses are for the larger size.
Gauge 3.5 sts = 1 inch
24" or 32" circular needles in size 8
Bulky weight yarn, preferably in a natural fiber—400 yards

Explanation of abbreviations used in patterns: Knitting patterns rely on a standard set of abbreviations to make the pattern directions as straightforward as possible. Below is an explanation of the terms used in my pattern.

k	knit
p	purl
st	stitch
sts	stitches

inc	increase
dec	decrease
cont	continue
k2tog TBL	knit two stitches together through the back side of the loop
p2tog TBL	purl two stitches together through the back side of the loop
* *	repeat instructions within * * as a recurring pattern

Body

Before you start, make certain you check your gauge. The pattern won't work properly unless you're getting exactly 3.5 stitches to the inch. Cast on 130 (140) stitches. Join into a circle, being very careful not to allow the stitches to twist, or you'll end up with a mobius-strip type thing, not a sweater.

Knit in the round (work the knit stitch every row and you'll end up with stockinette, as if you'd knit one row and then purled the next) for 12 inches, or until desired underarm of sweater.

To shape the arm holes and later, the neck, you'll now work in flat knitting fashion. To do so, you may switch to straight needles of the same size as the circular needles, or use the circular needles as if they were straight. Note that you'll now need to knit on the right side of the sweater and purl on the wrong side.

Shaping Arms and Shoulders

Place 65 (70) stitches on a holder; this will be the back of the sweater, which we'll return to later. With remaining 65 (70) stitches, work the following:

Bind off first st at beginning of next 2 rows.

Work the arm shaping as such:

Row 1 (right side): purl 1, knit 1, purl 1, then knit across row until 5 sts remain, K2tog TBL (Through Back Loop), purl 1, knit 1, purl 1.

Row 2 (wrong side): knit 1, purl 1, knit 1, then purl across row until 5 sts. remain, P2 tog, knit 1, purl 1, knit 1.

Cont in this fashion until you're reduced 7 stitches per side. You should have 51 (61) stitches left. Cont knitting without reducing number of sts, being careful to maintain ribbing at edges, until you reach a good place for the shoulder seam. The piece should measure approximately 7½" from the beginning of the armhole reduction.

Cast off 4 stitches at beginning of next 6 rows until center 27 (37) stitches remain. Work these stitches for two more rows and then cast off.

Repeat this process with the back of sweater. When two pieces are complete, sew the shoulder seams together where you made reductions for the shoulder. Note that the neck edge is meant to roll, as is the waistband of this sweater.

Index

afghans, 57, 85, 111
Africa, 140–48
animal toys, 82–83
Armenian immigrants, 87–88
artists, 112–13

Baim, Peg, 38–43, 56–57
balance, 87–88, 151
Barbor, Cary, 37
Basket Stitch, 110–11
Benson, Herbert, 37–38
Berlenbach, Betty, 99–108
Blauvelt, Marie, 43–45
brain physiology, 40–42
Brower, Cher, 152–54
Buddhism, 88, 97–98

Capitolo, Rosemary Porter, 90–91, 93
cashmere, 181
Catholicism, 177
celebrities, 22, 24, 113–14, 179, 184–85

Cellarer, 87
chaos into order, 103–4
charity, 94–96, 108
Christianity, 94
circular knitting. *See* round, knitting in the
communal life, 104, 186–87, 195, 202–3
Coppola, Sophia, 114
cotton, 178
creativity, 112–37
    and brain physiology, 40–43
    of designing, 137, 149
    power of, 48
    risks of, 20–25
Crespo, Clare, 114–26
crocheting, 115

Damskey, Karen, 179, 183–88
designing, 107, 137, 195
    See also patterns
dishcloths, 188

Elizabeth, Sr., 140–50
empowerment, 131, 149
Esmay, Judith, 105–8
expectations, 27

Fair, Georgia Howorth, 50–53
Falick, Melanie, 168
Fassett, Kaffe, 55, 136
feminism, 150–52
finishers, professional, 180–81
food, 114–26

Garter Stitch, 19, 198
George's Gallery, 122–23
gift-giving, 132
Gildersleeve, Mary C., 89
Grant, Alexandra (Xan).
   See Xan
group projects, 108
Gunn, Kathryn, 160

happiness, 56–57
Hart, Edna, 121
Harvard Medical School
   Mind/Body Medical Institute,
   37–38, 40
Hatfield, Anita, 165–66
Highland Hall School, 60–82
Holt, Cherryl, 161–62

illness, 160–66
intelligence, 27
Internet, 200
Irish Moss Stitch, 189
Islam, 94
Ison, Tara, 126–32

Jersey, 35, 198
Judaism, 94, 177
Jung, Carl, 104

Karadin, Becky, 163–64
Keene, Nietzchka, 132–37
Knit Stitch, Simple, 1
Knitters Magazine, 168
Knitting Guild of America, 203
Knitting in America (Falick), 168
knitting shops, 18, 135, 179–88,
   199–201

Lampe, Jean, 162
L'Atelier, 179–88
learning, 18, 52–53, 147–48,
   197–203
   See also Waldorf School
Lewinsky, Monica, 179, 184
linen, 177–78
Living Buddha, Living Christ
   (Thich Nhat Hanh), 47

McGowan, Rose, 126
McGrath, Karen, 162–63
meditation, 16–17
   and brain physiology, 41–43
   Buddhist concept of, 97
   and coping with illness, 90–92,
      160–61
   forms of, 36–39, 44–50
   and repetitive motions, 135
   sound, 173–74
metaphorical understanding of life,
   31–32, 104–5, 192–93
mittens, Latvian, 168–76

Mitzvah Day, 94–96
Montgolf, Kathy, 50
Morris, Shawn, 160
Moss Stitch, 139

Nairn, Ron, 36
needles, double-pointed, 201–2

occupations, 99, 104–5, 124–26,
    129–37, 148

Parker, Judith, 53–55
patterns
    alteration of, 147
    for beginners, 128, 205–8
    choosing, 199–200
    creation, 149
    made-to-order, 180
    See also designing
perfectionism, 32, 39, 162,
    187–88
planning, 49–50
practicality of knitting, 145–48
prayer, 87–92, 97–98, 102–3, 161
    See also spirituality
Preston Youth Correctional
    Facility, 165
pride, 131–32, 148
process, 49–50, 132, 187
Pullover, Sleeveless Rolled Neck,
    205–8
purl stitch, 198

relaxation response, 37–40, 43
Rice Stitch, 139
Rodman, Betsy, 154

round, knitting in the, 65, 80, 201,
    205–8
Rule of St. Benedict, 67, 87

scarves, 33–34, 111
Schwartz, Eugene, 65
The Secret Life of Food (Crespo),
    118
September 11 attacks, 190–96
Seward, Elizabeth, 62–74, 166,
    177–78
Sha'atnez, 177
silk, 178
Silver Lake, 112–13, 115
Simple Rib, 59
Simple Seed Stitch, 167
socks, 45–46
spirituality
    and art of silence, 149
    and brain physiology, 40–43
    and coping with pain, 108–9,
        165
    search for, 29–33
    through mindfulness of action,
        86, 101–5, 187
    See also meditation; prayer
St. Andrew's Abbey, 66–67
Steiner, Rudolf, 62, 64
Stockinette Stitch, 35, 198
Stormon, Leslie, 179–80,
    183–84
stress, 37–38
Strick, Candace Eisner, 154
Sue's Design, 126
sweaters, 106–8, 111, 128–29,
    157

tai chi, 173
taiji quan, 173
Taylor-Roberts, Nancy, 96–99
teaching, 18, 52–53, 147–48
    See also Waldorf School
therapy, 50–57, 160–66, 186
Thich Nhat Hanh, 47
time, 32–33, 51
Toth, Cecile Bewley, 49–50
trend, 125–26, 184–85
Trinity Stitch, 57, 85

Upitis, Lizbeth, 168–76
Urban, Linda, 170, 172

Vroman's Museum Collection
    shop, 169–70

Waffle-Stitch, 159
Walden, Anna, 55–56
*Waldorf Education: A Family
    Guide* (Schwartz), 65
Waldorf School, 60–82
    fifth graders, 66, 79–82
    first graders, 65, 74–79

walking, 87–88
washcloths, 188
Wasser, Emily, 154–55
Web sites, 200
What is Meditation (Nairn), 36
wisdom, 140–42, 152–57, 175
wool, 100–103, 177–78

Xan, 45–49

yarn
    acrylic, 46–47
    cashmere, 181
    color and texture, 69–70,
        135–37, 150
    making, 100–103, 106–8
    natural *vs.* synthetic, 176–78
    See also knitting shops

Zen Buddhism, 36